The Brides of March

The Brides of March

✦

Memoir of a Same-Sex Marriage

Beren deMotier

iUniverse, Inc.
New York Lincoln Shanghai

The Brides of March
Memoir of a Same-Sex Marriage

iUniverse books may be ordered through booksellers or by contacting:

iUniverse
2021 Pine Lake Road, Suite 100
Lincoln, NE 68512
www.iuniverse.com
1-800-Authors (1-800-288-4677)

The views expressed in this work are solely those of the author and do not necessarily reflect the views of the publisher, and the publisher hereby disclaims any responsibility for them.

The events detailed in this book are written from the author's memory; any factual or historical inaccuracies are entirely unintentional.

ISBN: 978-0-595-43987-4 (pbk)
ISBN: 978-0-595-88308-0 (ebk)

Printed in the United States of America

For Jannine

Contents

Acknowledgment

This book couldn't exist without the Brides of March: Chris, Lisa, Marty, Terri, Jeanna, Ellen, Cindy, and Teri, the women who made the marriages possible: Diane Linn, Maria Rojo de Steffey, Serena Cruz, Lisa Naito, and Roey Thorpe, the man who married us, Associate Minister Tom Disrud of the First Unitarian Church, Portland, Oregon, and all the friends and family who offered their help and blessings, especially Laurie and Jason, human beings extraordinaire. Thank you, Bonnie, for editing out my howlers, the Doubletree Hotel Lloyd Center for giving me shelter during rewrites, and Toyota for making the Sienna minivan in which this book was written during naptime. Thanks also to my grandfather, David Duncan, who showed me you don't have to choose between art and writing, and to my kids, who taught me what life was all about.

Cover photo by H. Jannine Setter.
Author photo by H. Jannine Setter.

Preface

As a little girl, I didn't dream of getting married someday with a Cinderella dress and six matching bridesmaids in puce. I didn't put lace tablecloths over my head and weave up imaginary aisles clutching a dozen dying daisies. I didn't even have any predictable wedding fantasies for a child of the sixties, like imagining myself a barefoot princess in a white hippie dress, marrying the handsome (if long-haired) prince, and living happily ever after, maybe in a commune. My one childhood foray into marriage fantasy was when I became briefly engaged to a pleasantly plump, easy-going boy named Douglas in kindergarten. It was Los Angeles, fall of 1969, and we planned to marry on roller skates, which seemed ever so important at the time.

Admittedly, I was not exactly force fed bridal veil, lacy gown, packed pews, and Tiffany & Company romance at home. My mother was married in her parents' backyard with a gold band, a handful of her parents' friends, and a simple off-white lace cocktail dress. Years later, she buried this classy number on the beach next to the charred remains of every single one of her wedding pictures.

My one adolescent wedding fantasy focused on marrying for money while wearing a red satin strapless gown a` la Rita Hayworth as *Gilda*, because I had a lot more faith in my figure than in love. Marrying a man for love just didn't come into it; which made sense when I came out as a lesbian (as did the fact that my Barbie doll tended to kick Ken across the room and hang out with that babe, Malibu P.J., instead); and marrying a woman for love was not an option.

In 1983, gay marriage was unthinkable, legally or symbolically. It simply wasn't done.

It wasn't until my spouse and I had spent years living in sin that commitment ceremonies became common and marriage moved from my unconscious back burner to the front of the stove on high. I got wedding fever, wanting desperately to marry the woman I loved, not just for the legal rights, but for the chance to say "I do" with feeling.

Being very able at accessorizing, I developed a whole scenario involving a voluminous white skirt, barefoot children running around, green grass, white flowers and, in some versions, a baby in my arms. My spouse, bless her pragmatic heart, had no fantasies in the marriage department other than if it became legal, she wanted to do it. In the end, we both had some of our dreams come true.

This is the story I hope to be telling grandchildren years from now, about the day my wife and I were married in a short, sweet, extemporaneous church wedding, on a rainy Wednesday morning in March, with nary a skirt in sight.

By then, I trust, this story will have a different ending.

The Brides of March

March 2nd, 2004

The phone rang just after six o'clock. It was Tuesday night, and Jannine had just edged her way through the front door with a guitar case on either side of her, coming home from lessons with our nine year-old daughter, Anna, a compact-model blonde who looked too young to be playing electric guitar, as well as acoustic. They were taking lessons together, our daughter learning an interesting juxtaposition of "Zip-a-dee-doo-da" and "I Don't Give a Damn 'Bout my Bad Reputation", while Jannine was still working on "This Land is Your Land", strumming away in her office after the rest of us had gone to bed, the tune reverberating through the floor, through my brain, and musically scoring my dreams.

I'd just come home from a swimming lesson with our two sons. At twelve, Duncan definitely fell on the smaller end of the height/weight scale, his brain far outdistancing his body. He was the swimmer, lessons just building on the skills he'd already earned with two summers on swim team. His brother, Graeme, had just turned one (a virtual carbon copy of his siblings, though on a grander scale), but while his enthusiasm for water raised my alert level to orange, he was a little young for actual swim lessons.

We were all exhausted, burned out from a marathon season of back-to-school, first head cold, Halloween, second head cold, Duncan's birthday, relatives to stay, third head cold, travel to Seattle for Thanksgiving, influenza for four, pneumonia for two, Jannine's parents visiting pre-Christmas, my relatives visiting for Christmas, our anniversary (during which we learned that Jannine's dad was in the hospital after a blood clot passed through his heart), Jannine rushing to Seattle to see her dad, fourth head cold, New Year's Eve, a record breaking snowfall closing school for a week, fifth head cold, Anna's birthday, relatives to stay, sixth head cold, Graeme's birthday, Valentine's Day, and then the inevitable parental breakdown we suffer every late February, when we lie on the floor, our bodies twitching, and shake our heads while repeating, "No more … no more … no more …" September through February that year was a pharmaceutically enhanced blur.

1

We were numbly looking forward to an evening of take-home pizza and the movie, *School of Rock*. Then, the phone rang. Our friend and across the street neighbor, Terri, had news. Her partner Marty's eighty-one year-old mother had just called to say that Multnomah County, our county, was going to start issuing marriage licenses to same-sex couples at ten o'clock the following morning.

The movie forgotten, my spouse became a woman possessed, and the always lingering birth certificate issue raised its ugly head. I didn't have one—long story involving an irresponsible youth, family-of-origin trauma-drama, a long delayed legal name change, and snail mail gone astray. Not having any compelling reason to possess a birth certificate (international travel seemed unlikely with three kids and a modest budget), I had passive-aggressively avoided doing anything about it. But now, it was a problem. Always preferring to search the World Wide Web in lieu of speaking to a message machine or an actual human being, Jannine started surfing. Did we need birth certificates to get a marriage license? Did we need to prove residency? Was there a waiting period or could we get married immediately after getting a license? How many pieces of picture ID would suffice? Not finding what she wanted, she started calling people.

Jannine is a jeans and T-shirt, step out of the shower and go, straight shooter kind of gal. She was once asked to describe herself in ten words or less at a job interview, gave it a moment's thought, counted on her fingers and responded, "What you see is what you get." She wasn't afraid to roust people from the dinner table. Our straight married friends were no help; they'd filled out their licenses on auto-pilot. Jannine called Terri back.

"I'm going down to the County Building to see if they have any applications available in the lobby, do you want to go?"

Terri was slipping on her winter coat and out the door in a heartbeat; she and Marty, co-moms of their daughter, McKenzie, had been together sixteen years. Before I could even explain to Duncan and Anna our change of plans for the evening, Jannine and Terri were in our white minivan and gone.

Before they'd gone three blocks, Jannine said, "Let's go get Chris."

Chris and her spouse, Lisa, are close friends whose two children are like siblings to ours. Chris, like Jannine, is "the boy-mom," adept at power tool use and able to window shop for hours at Home Depot (or rationalize large purchases) when she's not working eighty hours a week as a professor of nursing. Lisa, while toting the emotional baggage and hairstyle of a "girl mom," is just as capable of wielding a drill or a router; she just knows Chris wants to more. Lisa (a.k.a. "She Who Must Be Obeyed") is also the nurse midwife who both talked me off the ceiling, and caught Graeme on his way into the world; she made his worrying birth a time punctuated by frequent laughter, as well as guttural growls of agony.

When Lisa opened the door to Terri and Jannine, she was giddy. All pretense of detached rationality was gone. Their phone had been ringing off the hook as friends called them to tell them the news and ask, "Are you going to get married?" Thrilled as they were, they were still planning on watching a movie with their kids (was Tuesday night movie night in every house in the neighborhood?), and Chris was at her desk, working as usual. Jannine and Terri put a stop to that, telling Lisa they would literally drag Chris from her third floor office, out the door, and all the way to the County Building should she put up any resistance.

Chris didn't put up much of a fight.

It Was the Colored Contact Lenses that Brought Us Together

Seattle, November, 1986

"Who are you?" I asked the girl who'd set her motorcycle helmet on the counter where I was working, raking her up and down with my eyes. She was clearly not a customer (or I'd have been all attention, no attitude) and knew me; her china blue eyes eager and friendly, her lopsided smile expectant, innocent of the knowledge that her straight brown hair was stuck "helmet-head" to her skull. I searched the mental rolodex, coming up empty. Where in the world would I have encountered this woman I would later describe as wholesome as a warm slice of wheat bread?

Not that I wasn't used to strange women coming into the poster and framing store where I worked, thinking they knew me. Sometimes, they would just cruise the card racks, peek over and leave. Other times, they would linger, and when I asked if I could help them, they'd snicker, "Weren't you naked the last time I saw you?" a by-product of dancing in a red lace g-string in front of four hundred lesbians in a bar.

"I'm Jannine," she said, "Kelline's friend." It came back to me in pieces; my ex-girlfriend at Tugs Belltown, a long, narrow, brick-lined dive, standing with her ostensibly straight best friend, Jannine; me dancing against the brick wall to "Missionary Man" by the Eurythmics, rubbing my ego on the crowd. I had thought it would be fun to scare the straight girl, cozying up to her at the bar, enjoying her blushes. She hadn't forgotten me.

The excuse for interrupting me at work was a gift for Kelline. I'd known her longer, Jannine wanted my advice. She found excuses to show up a few more times over the next couple weeks as she finished up her Bachelor of Science at the University of Washington, and December found me riding to a mutual friend's house on the back of her motorcycle.

Never mind that I was dating someone else (who I later learned was already dating someone else), or that Jannine was supposedly straight as a board, or that her best buddy wanted me back, she kept showing up.

Jannine was a nice girl, a junior varsity rower, the manager of a Little Caesar's pizza restaurant, and a former high school softball player whose mother still picked out her clothes. She was on the fast track from undergrad to grad school to business career to please her parents. She'd been a Coast Guard military brat, moving from school to school across the continental U.S., able to say goodbye without looking back, or hello without meaning it, and not good at putting down roots.

I graduated from the University of Washington that summer with a Bachelor of Arts in Women's Studies (useless monetarily, but emotionally liberating), helped manage the poster store days, and spent my nights hovering on the fringe of the cool people I'd somehow infiltrated on the platform at Tugs: professional dancers who invited me to perform with them in their erotic shows for women, S/M dykes who invited me to model backless skirts in leather fashion shows, and pretty people who invited me to hang out. Not having grown up and out of the adolescent desire to be cool, I accepted all the invitations and more.

We were twenty-two.

Shortly before Christmas, Jannine drove Kelline and me in her beat up old Jeep Wagoneer to get a Christmas tree. It was while we were piling into the car, getting ready to go, that Kelline leaned over the front seat and said, "I had the weirdest dream last night about you guys. It was years from now, and you two were together, and had a house, and all these kids."

What could we say to such an outrageous idea?

At the Christmas tree lot, it started drizzling. Jannine was along for the ride, grabbing any tree I showed interest in, holding it up for inspection. She was walking backward, keeping her eyes on me as we made our way down the line of trees, the day rapidly turning to night. There was something in the way she smiled as she held up the third tree she'd wrestled from the pile of evergreens. I stopped looking at the tree, and looked into her eyes instead. The drizzle turned to snow. The lights surrounding the tree lot twinkled. She bit her lip nervously. I told her, "You have the bluest eyes." We both held our breaths, time stood still, and we were falling.

I only later discovered that she wore colored contacts.

Then run, rabbit, run, by New Year's Day she was gone, driving the three thousand miles with her brother back to Embry Riddle Aeronautical University in Florida, for graduate school—the Jeep breaking down in Mississippi along the way—leaving me with no guarantees.

For me, it was love, which might not have stopped me from doing my best to blow it, going back to dating people I should have been smart enough to avoid, and generally exploiting myself before someone else could do it for me, except for my friend, Tiger. It was Tiger, a runaway baby dyke, who made me ready for Jannine. Tiger, who in November took off her leather jacket, folded it neatly on the cement outside the door of the Capitol Hill Alano Club, laid her glasses carefully on top, sat down cross-legged beside them, and in a seventeen year-old moment of darkness and determination, blew her brains out with a hand gun.

Tiger was a permeable girl, boundary-less, and longing to be loved. Despite obvious differences: college grad versus high school drop-out, self-supporting versus public assistance, we had a lot in common. Without recognizing her other assets (her smile, her wit, her good nature, her optimism in the face of heavy odds), she offered her body in order to please. But when she tried to crawl into my bed one late summer night when she'd been kicked out by her latest, I said, "No." She was incredulous that I wouldn't accept her offer, her one gift, and in that moment, my paradigm shifted, and I felt a maternal instinct to protect her young soul, and mine.

I hadn't seen her for a couple of months before she died. She was doing OK, I thought, trying to get her GED, dating girls her own age, instead of adults who knew better, but then her optimism failed her. I couldn't save her young soul from further harm, but maybe I could save my own.

Jannine, plunging into graduate school in Daytona Beach, was terrified. She had done everything she could to avoid love and dating and romance. She hadn't had high school boyfriends, or even noticed the softball girls who tried to get her attention. Her team mates on the women's rowing team at the UW (several of whom had been evicted from another university during a witch hunt for homosexuals) scared her to death with their bravado and sheer brute strength. She did nothing in the dating department, so she wouldn't have to face whether she could come out or not. Her mother had raised her to believe that being gay meant a life of shame and sorrow. The dating antics among her lesbian friends at college seemed silly and shallow. She is, and was, an all or nothing gal. She wanted to be sure that what we felt was love, which meant all the trappings: in-laws, the picket fence, children, barbeques with the neighbors, and a joint checking account or she didn't want any part of it.

I don't know what she saw in me. From that first "Who are you?" she should have run. She could have used a million excuses to let "us" go. But, she didn't.

I have been a chameleon over time: barefoot hippie nature child, high school theatre geek, bisexual stoner babe, radicalesbianfeminist undergrad, erotic-dancer wanna-be, and finally, stay-at-home mom. Jannine has remained much the same. She started out as a girl who wanted to wear jeans and tennis shoes every day, not giving a hoot about appearances or gender appropriate clothing. She is just the same at forty, though her original narrow worldview has grown wide. At the same age, I have somehow gone full circle. I am the nature child again, the one who used to go barefoot on the barnacled rocks on Vancouver Island, showing the tourists where to dig for clams while my long hair whipped around my shoulders; though today, I would do the same wearing lipstick, and my heels are cracked from decades of less than sensible shoes.

If there is something that made us stick, besides the stars, sheer stubbornness, and a synchronicity we could never have planned, it would be our values. Values seem silly when they are hauled around like so much baggage by pundits and politicians. But, they aren't. Values are what make us who we are, even ex-erotic dancer wanna-bes and the women who love them. Underneath Jannine's doesn't-give-a-hoot exterior is a fierce dedication to family, to stability, to a middle-class lifestyle she aspires to, not because she wants the coolest toys in town, but because she wants to keep money worries to a minimum, and to offer her children the same opportunities her parents gave her. Her long hours aren't about avoiding family life or keeping up with Bob in the next cubicle; it's a dedication to doing the job right.

Like Jannine, I worked my way through college: but when we had Duncan, the real hard work began. I was overtaken by a drive to do the best by our kids. Though the best doesn't mean a spotless home, all the extracurricular classes money can buy, life as a chauffeur, or bedrooms that belong in the pages of magazines; it means sitting down to dinner together every night and homemade Halloween costumes. It means reading aloud, talking about dinosaurs until I am blue in the face, making the library a second home—but not doing the kids' homework for them. The laundry is often undone. The dishes sometimes sit overnight. But we do our best to get the kids to bed happily and unrushed every night, putting sleep first, so they are ready for another day.

The Grooms Get the License

When Jannine, Chris, and Terri tumbled out of the van at the Multnomah County Building, the door was locked, even to the lobby. No forms were available. There was no one inside the building and no one else there, except a conspicuous line of news vans jockeying for position at the curb, staking out their spots for the next morning. When the first reporter saw Chris, Terri, and Jannine standing at the door, wondering what to do next, she bounded up with a microphone.

"Are you the first ones in line?"

They glanced at each other, smiled, and answered as one, "Yes, we are."

Chris shared her cell phone all around as "the brides" were called (apparently grooms get the license, an arcane piece of wedding etiquette I had no previous opportunity to learn), and when Jannine had her turn, her first words were, "I'm staying."

She went on, "Call Marty and Lisa, they're bringing down sleeping bags and supplies, you can send stuff with them. Maybe the big kids can come, too? Could you find the port-a-potty? Chris thinks we'll need it, you know, three middle-aged women ... and can you remember my camera?"

Stunned at the turn of events, I shifted Graeme to my other hip and made a list on the nearest scrap of paper. "OK, I'll call them," I assured her.

She hung up, only to call back a moment later. "By the way, in case I didn't ask you earlier, will you marry me?"

"Yes," I told her, "I will."

She had asked me before, months earlier. When same-sex marriage in British Columbia was announced publicly, within minutes, a ripple of matrimonial momentum swept through our circle of friends, partners phoning each other to propose at the first opportunity: at lunch breaks, via e-mail, by text message on pagers. Jannine skipped that romantic component and went straight to making potential travel plans, not bothering to ask. When I chided her about it, she went down on one knee and asked me to be her wife.

I think, in my heart of hearts, I'd wanted a wedding from the moment I knew she was the one, but only dared acknowledge it when we had a track record to back up such an audacious desire. Somewhere during these years together, we could have found someone to perform a ceremony and rustled up some folks to attend; we even had our own ring-bearer living in situ, and later a flower girl (who would have grooved on the whole thing), but it wouldn't have been a real wedding, with sincere support and the blessings of friends, family, and community.

At least, that's what Jannine said, and I never convinced her otherwise (and I tried), possibly, because I knew she was right.

If you bring home your true love of the opposite sex, there's a good chance that your family will welcome him or her with open arms, glad either that you are happy, or to finally get you off their hands. With a same-sex true love, there's a good chance that ten years into the relationship, one of you will be getting that "are you still here?" look when both of you arrive for any family function. Jannine didn't want to celebrate our union when the guests might arrive with serious reservations about the whole thing.

And Jannine has wedding issues. The fuss about minutiae (cream versus ecru, bridesmaid shoes dyed to match, effigies made with marzipan) and the sexist rituals (the garter bit, the crude jokes about the wedding night, the "me, me, throw it to me" bridal bouquet toss) do nothing for her. Over the years, with friends or family, she's heard too often how many dollars each catered meal costs, seen one too many photographs of piled up wedding plunder, and attended more than her share of weddings which ended in divorce before the wedding debt was paid off.

I guess it took all the romance out of it for her.

But I've yearned. I've cried in the silver section of department stores, and I'm not especially fond of silver. For years, I couldn't look at a bridal registry sheet without misting up, glanced avariciously at the window of the wedding boutique on Northwest Twenty-third, and yes, I'd have almost converted to some sort of religion just to be able to marry. Heterosexuality, however, wasn't among the religions I was willing to join.

The years rolled on, social and family tolerance became acceptance, acceptance became celebration, and by the time we had a circle of family and friends who might sincerely cheer at our nuptials, it had been a long, long time. As my father-in-law, Jon, likes to say about his married years, "Time flies when you're having fun."

Without a specific reason to marry—like the hundreds of rights and privileges legal marriage offers—the whole thing seemed pretty moot.

But then, legal marriage started being an option, first in British Columbia, and then Massachusetts was moving fast in that direction, and suddenly, Mayor Gavin Newsom was marrying same-sex couples in San Francisco on Valentine's Day. It was tempting to fly down and take part in the celebration. But, it didn't seem real. Lisa put it best when a friend asked her whether she and Chris were going to get married in Canada, and Lisa said, "No!" with emphatic hand gestures, if she were going to get married, she wanted to do it in her community, in her church, in her country. Jannine and I hadn't thought it out so succinctly, but we hadn't made a move to marry elsewhere, despite initial urges to emigrate north. We had been holding our breath, I think, with a hope and a prayer that it could happen here, rather than in Canada, or San Francisco, or Massachusetts. And it was. We had no idea this was coming. But, none of us hesitated. As Jannine said later, "Who would have expected three middle-aged women to be the first on that dime?"

Just When I'd Given Up on Marriage

It is ironic that this window of marital opportunity opened just when I'd finally become at peace with closing the door to being a bride (though I will never be at peace with being a lesser couple in the eyes of the law). I was even able to attend a wedding last year without batting an eye.

Previously hyperventilating and needing therapy every time another friend or relative headed to the altar, I turned the corner three years ago when my cousin, Leah, got married. We arrived home unscathed after a whirlwind tour of St. Louis and Relative City, complete with Hebrew, high heels, beautiful, but basically inedible cake, and the obligatory negative experience with a distant relation.

Luckily, it was the groom's distant relation, not mine, and just a ghastly faux pas that only Jannine was privy to.

We arrived at my aunt's house after eight hours of relentless parental vigilance over our then six and nine year-old children during taxi rides, air flight, airport shuttles, car rental paperwork, and hotel registration confusion—"You want two king beds? But where will the children sleep?" I'd had an hour's sleep the night before, and not enough food, so I was useless. Therefore, it was Jannine who sprang upstairs to check on our children, who were being treated to the delights of Playstation Two by my cousin, Dov, just to make sure they weren't seeing any decapitations. As Jannine walked by, she heard this callow young man talking on the phone about what a drag it was when you have a wedding and you're obligated to invite all these distant relatives, when you'd rather have those invites for friends (apparently clueless that the gathering downstairs was arranged specifically for the extended family members who had come into town for the big event).

My spouse, travel fatigued and the keeper of the family budget, managed to not turn on him savagely, rip the phone from his insensitive hand and tell him that those distant relatives then felt obligated to spend a thousand dollars to get there, in order to wish the couple well. She showed great restraint in the circumstances.

And really, we wanted to go. We are very fond of my cousin, love her mother dearly, and our children danced into the wee hours, played with candle wax and ate multiple pieces of cake.

They like weddings.

It was nice not spending the whole time yearning for my own wedding. I didn't feel even the slightest hint of envy for the bridal role, nor did I want my weight in toaster ovens, or even a honeymoon in Hawaii.

All right, maybe Hawaii.

I'm sure Jannine was relieved. I'd wanted a wedding for years, needed it, it was a cleaver in my heart. But it was gone. Maybe, I finally believed that she loved me.

Not that attending weddings has been all pain, no gain, we've gotten a lot of emotional mileage out of family weddings. Because of them, Jannine knows my unique and preposterous extended family, including my Great Aunt Joyce, who writes humorous poetry about, among other things, multiple piercing; and I've been enveloped warmly by the Eastern Washington branch of her family, who accepted me as a breeding mare of exceptional quality.

It was at my other cousin Maddy's wedding, a few years back, that my mother and I had an emotional breakthrough. We were in that seeming eternity between ceremony and reception that is meant to be a mix, mingle, and drink time, but for me, was a panic attack waiting to happen, since I don't drink and my mingling needs work. My mother and I found ourselves standing together in the garden court, smiling as Maddy blew kisses from rooms above, running from window to window, radiant and joyous. Turning, I saw Maddy's mother chatting with her new son-in-law's parents, her ex-husband by her side, an affectionate hand on her back. They were there for their daughter.

"That's my wish," I told my mother, "I want us to be family, for you and Jannine's parents to come together when there are moments like these. To let differences not matter, and just be happy for us."

Our mothers hadn't had a good start as in-laws, partly because they were a lesson in opposites: Republican versus Democrat, married versus divorced, stay-at-home mother versus working mom, high school graduate versus University of California, Berkeley, graduate program. They met at our baby shower, when both of them weren't most at ease: my mother because a baby shower for her lesbian daughter wasn't quite within her original frame of reference, and Jannine's because her first grandchild had disappeared with his father the day before during a visitation, and Grandma was crackling with anxiety, awaiting his eventual safe return. That had been six years before, and the mothers had been politely distant, and sat at opposite sides of the room if they had to be in the same room at all, ever since.

My mother didn't say anything then, at Maddy's wedding, but she soon worked to make my wish come true. Jannine's mom and dad met her halfway. It was a memorable evening when the two moms sat in our living room regaling us with stories about being poor in the fifties, the cheap crinolines they wore under their dresses, the humiliating lessons in posture they had to endure, and the ways they managed to be fashionable on nothing. The highlight was when both grandmothers told us we should get on with it and have more kids.

So, we had Graeme.

Supplying the Troops

"Why is marriage so important to you that you are camping all night to get a license?" "What makes you want to go through a legal marriage ceremony?" "Where will you get married when you get your license?" "Will you rush right out, or wait to plan a wedding?"

Chris, Terri, and Jannine fielded all of the above and more, Chris often taking the "this is an important legal step, not just for us, but for all gay people seeking the right to marriage" angle in her calm, reasonable, radio-ready tones; Terri the "this is about equality" stand in emphatic, forthright, and eminently quotable sentences; and Jannine responding in her usual folksy style that she deserves "the same rights and privileges as any Oregonian, and the same protections for our children," and that she was there to make her relationship at long last legal.

I wasn't doing my own job of protecting our children too well at the time. I let Duncan and Anna go ahead and watch the movie *School of Rock* by themselves, hoping blindly that Jack Black wouldn't do anything too risqué. I stuck Graeme in the baby backpack, which he tolerates with good grace, and headed to the basement to look for the port-a-potty accompanied by our enormous Labrador, who nervously shadowed my every move, his body language saying, "What's up? What's up? What's up?"

Would it really happen? I hoisted the port-a-potty up the stairs, checked that there was a bucket and a plastic bag inside, and set it by the front door. Would we really be able to get a license and get married? I shoved a dozen nutrition bars into a freezer bag. Would there be an injunction before we could have our seventeen-year union recognized? The camping area next, water bottles, sleeping bags ...

Could this all be real? Would we really, in the eyes of the law, be married? The camera, I had to remember the camera!

There was a heap by the door when Marty knocked, ready to transport young humans and gear to the County Building.

"Can you believe it?" were her first words when I opened the door. Like me, she had a wild-eyed expression that signaled joy, hope, doubt, and shock all in one.

It was oh-so fitting that Marty's mom gave them the news, because Marty knows everything first. If you want to know how to get somewhere, not only will she know where it is, she will remember the exact route, the exit numbers, the mileage, and an alternative route. She's an obsessive newspaper reader who can analyze both political policy and the personal history of the guy who lives down the street with equal ease, and is hopelessly addicted to the obituaries.

Her partner, Terri, has the calm competence that made her the one we ran to when Duncan slammed a metal screen door on his finger years ago, the fingernail punching through to the other side, knowing she would take him through the obligatory clean-up kindly. She offers assistance with splinters, head knocks, and obscure medical conditions, her heart always in the right place.

Their daughter, McKenzie, appeared in the doorway, muffled up to the eyeballs for the weather, "Are we ready to go now?" A take-no-prisoners girl with a mind of her own and chestnut ringlets, she wanted to be in on the action. Duncan and Anna pulled on coats and hats, and fairly flew down the front steps to the sidewalk. We squeezed the camping port-a-potty and our pile into the back of their already stuffed van (chairs, coolers, blankets, a laptop?) and Graeme and I waved as they drove off.

It felt anti-climactic to send the kids off with Marty, and wrong to not join Jannine in line, but a happy and well-rested baby comes first, especially if you might get married in the morning. Achieving happy and well-rested could be challenging, I knew, since Graeme was newly weaned, and I had no idea what the night might hold.

I'd cold turkey'd him at six o'clock the previous morning, one precious last feeding before buttoning up the milk source. It was a hard decision, but seemed necessary since sleep deprivation was getting to me both physically and psychologically, and fast becoming expensive. The previous week, I'd run into a pole at the video return box, putting a five hundred dollar dent in our new minivan, then inadvertently written a bad check to the orthodontist (wrong checking account), and couldn't for the life of me figure out why the check had bounced.

While I am the kind of mother who would happily nurse her offspring up to the preschool years, I told myself (with the emotional support of some good friends) that I needed to be a good mother not just to number three, but to numbers one and two as well, and I needed a brain for that.

This weaning thing is not just emotionally challenging, but logistically as well. He screamed himself silly for forty minutes the previous evening at bedtime (while furiously trying to pull up my T-shirt), before collapsing across my body, exhausted from his tirade. I'd sent everyone else to another floor of the house so they could sleep in peace. From experience, I knew he would survive this. I believed it was crueler to wean him bit by bit: "Will she nurse me now, or later? When will it be time? Where did the milk go? Why is she messing with my mind?" I could tell that when he screamed he wasn't terrified, or anguished, or deeply in sorrow. He was mad. So I held him, and soothed him, and steadfastly refused to lift my shirt. I'd done this before.

From Wonder Woman to One-Breasted Wonder

When I first dove into motherhood, like many women, I thought I should be Wonder Woman. I could have a baby on my hip, a pen in my hand, and a vacuum ... I don't even want to speculate. And nothing should be easy, either: no disposables, no baby-sitters, no playpens, cribs, or bottles of formula. I would nurture our babies at the breast, with antibodies, and proteins, and the very elixir of life.

Which was why I was a one-breasted wonder. Not that I wasn't lucky enough to still have two breasts, it's just that you couldn't tell by looking at me. One was gargantuan, like the breast of a Mesopotamian fertility goddess. The other was wasted away like the aging inside of a size-two society matron's ball gown.

Graeme was a left breast baby, like his sister before him.

Before childrearing, the functional capacity of breasts had never particularly interested me. They were a thing unto themselves: sensual, velvety, associated with college dorm rooms, and Geena Davis walking around in her underwear in *Tootsie*. The only thing I knew about my own breasts was that I wore the same bra size as Madonna and that they evoked interest from others.

All that changed with Duncan. From the moment Doctor Clark placed his newly born body on mine, his chief occupation was remaining attached to my breasts, night and day, day and night. There is a certain *je ne sais quoi* about the lactation period: their little hands holding you in a vise-like grip lest you get away before they take their fill, that sweet, drunken look they get as they latch on, and the knowledge that even if you are sitting on your butt reading a book while nursing, you are accomplishing an important task that no one but you can do.

I had been looking forward to the lactation lifestyle once more. I wouldn't have done it any other way. But babies have a way of their own. While Duncan wouldn't have left a drop un-drunk, both Anna and Graeme had a favorite side, and like any connoisseurs, would not be swayed. Anna was eight months old when she switched, and she may not have been able to speak, but she made herself perfectly clear. Upon being placed against the wrong breast, she faked it for a minute and then hurled herself to the other side, rubbing her face determinedly against my left side until I let her in.

Graeme seemed to come out of the womb with his predilection, which after weeks of lactation consultation, we discovered was wise on his part. The left side was like sucking through a milk shake straw, the right like sipping through a clogged coffee stir, unproductive and energy consuming. No wonder Anna and Graeme gave it up. The results were my lop-sided situation. When I told the pediatrician years ago that Anna would only nurse on one side, she replied "Obviously," and I still had my coat on. Jannine had failed to notice anything until I mentioned the pediatrician's comment, at which time she blinked, gaped and said, "Whoa!" So much for her powers of observation.

With Anna, I wondered if it was Mother Nature's way of giving my right breast a much needed vacation after Duncan, or if it was symbolic of an over-abundance on my analytical side, and an undernourished creative one. With Graeme, I know it must have been my Wonder Woman complex; I was so powerful I could feed an infant with one breast tied behind my back.

Not even Wonder Woman could do that.

First in Line

"Goin' to the chapel, and we're gonna get married," sang Chris and Terri in unison, complete with finger snapping and swaying hips, as television cameramen smiled and filmed it all. They followed that up with a rousing rendition of "I'm Getting Married in the Morning," the song nearly complete when their children ran screaming down the sidewalk and literally leapt on them, after Lisa and Marty released them from their respective vans.

The kids were buzzed, almost as thrilled as the moms at this sudden turn of events, and with much more energy. Anna clung like a monkey to Katie, and Duncan and Jacob quickly got down to the business of discussing Dungeons and Dragons, their latest enthusiasm, and one that I met with anxiety, having dated two practitioners of the game: one within the normal range of gaming geekdom, and one who would disappear for days at a time to play and consume copious amounts of drugs and alcohol.

Jacob, like Duncan, is intense, though his comes in the volcanic format and Duncan's in the hidden riptide, and his large, green eyes shaded by thick lashes are a reminder of his likeness to a Renaissance Jesus in infancy. Katie was, at thirteen, the perfect older girl idol for Anna, a charming combination of Ethel Merman, Hilary Clinton, and Amy March from *Little Women*, unblushing in her selfhood.

"Do we have to go to school tomorrow?" McKenzie asked, voicing the unspoken question the kids wanted answered.

Marty and Terri looked at her like she was crazy, "No way, you've got a wedding to go to!" creating a spontaneous cheer among the kids at the thought that not only were their parents going to get married, they got to miss a day of school as well.

Eminently practical, Lisa pointed out that even if they didn't have to go to school, they did have to go to bed, so the kids were hustled back into the vans, waving one last time at the cameramen and reporters, before being driven first to our house, so they could see themselves on the eleven o'clock news and fill me in on all the details.

"There's something going on outside the Multnomah County Building," the news anchorwoman said as the local news started, and the kids piled themselves onto our family room floor, Marty and Lisa collapsing on the couch. Graeme was still awake, determined not to miss anything, yet remarkably cheerful considering his routine was upset, his people scattered, and his breast milk mysteriously denied him. The news cameras showed that the line had extended beyond the other two couples who had joined our crew, ready to camp all night, and that others were arriving steadily. Already, the strange contrast between reality and spin was evident, as the news anchor described the "ongoing drama," and the cameras clearly indicated that what was happening couldn't have been less dramatic.

The night brought little sleep for Chris, Terri, and Jannine. Jannine came home for a couple of hours around midnight to work, finishing tasks due, and sending out an e-mail to her boss and co-workers to say she wouldn't be in the next day because she hoped to be getting married. Chris tried to sleep in our van, stretching out to ease the pain from her recently broken leg. Terri didn't even try to rest. She sat on her lawn chair next to our friend Jeanna, who had joined "the grooms" in line. They chatted with the next women behind them, and whoever came up to them during the night.

From midnight on, supporters brought coffee, donuts, and flowers. Members of *Love Makes a Family*, a gay and lesbian family advocacy group, made regular visits to make sure the couples had everything they needed, and felt safe.

The reporters were there for the duration, asking questions of anyone who was willing to be quoted, and not necessarily getting it that the first three women in line had spouses awaiting them at home, resulting in continuous errors as to who was marrying whom. In various reports, Chris was marrying Jannine, Jannine was marrying Terri, and Terri was marrying Chris, unnatural combinations that would never work. It got too tiring, and time consuming, for the three of them to correct all the misimpressions, and every couple later received at least one congratulatory card addressed to the wrong set of spouses.

There was also the "are you the first in line?" question. All three tried to explain that they all were first in line, and each had that spot at some point during the night. But the reporters wanted sound bites and the explanation was lost. Chris offered Bonnie Tinker, the head of *Love Makes a Family*, and her partner of twenty-seven years, Sara Graham, "first in line" status, in honor of their long commitment. It made a simpler sound bite, too.

I'd finally scraped the kids off the ceiling around midnight, settling them on the floor in our room. The expected tussle with Graeme was nonexistent. He was so exhausted he simply collapsed in my arms. I couldn't sleep, my mind racing, but I didn't dare get up and, I don't know—clean the house, do my nails, wax my upper lip? For fear that Graeme would wake up and scream the house down. I finally fell asleep after four, and was wakened at 5:10 when Jannine called, a catch of excitement in her voice:

"This is your wake-up call! You need to get down here. You and the kids need to be a part of this."

Luckily, Graeme was hard asleep, his irrepressible instinct to wake and follow me squashed by sheer fatigue. I hustled around in the half-light, brushed my hair, slapped on my face (lipstick, rouge, mascara, and three coats of under-eye concealer, including a touch of Preparation H to reduce the baggies), equivocated about clothing for thirty seconds, and woke the kids. They sprang up with a vengeance, jumped into their clothes without prompting, brushed teeth, combed hair, and were ready to go, a miracle of efficiency that paid tribute to their enthusiasm for this venture. We called Marty across the street (who was already up, moving, and making coffee), stuffed Graeme into his car seat still asleep, and managed to join our spouses by 6:15.

The line of couples was to the corner of the Multnomah County Building and beyond, a sea of spouses with one mission. Jannine was right by the double glass doors at the entrance when we reached her, with an *Oregonian* photographer standing beside her, waiting for developments.

"I need you to fill out your portion," Jannine handed me a marriage license application she'd been given in the night by *Love Makes a Family*, who'd stored up copies for just such an occasion. "Don't change anything or they'll make you start all over," she turned away to check on the older two kids, tickled Graeme who was now awake, then turned back, "Oh, and good morning," she said, kissing me.

A box of donuts was handed to us for the kids, and a man came by with trays of steaming Venti coffees from Starbucks. I declined, fearing an aneurysm if I got any more excited than I already was, though that didn't keep me from the Diet Coke I'd stuck in my bag.

"My partner and I got married in San Francisco, and someone brought us coffee, so I wanted to do the same for you," the man told us. After he moved down the line with the coffee, fresh glazed Krispy Kreme donuts made the circuit on a trolley pushed by a jubilant gay man, hocking donuts like a peanut vendor at a ball game, but without remuneration.

A multi-color haired, twenty-something was jumping up and down in place with excitement as she watched the line forming, squealing, "Oh my god, oh my god, oh my god, this is so exciting!"

A middle-aged straight man came up to Terri with a bottle of champagne. "I saw you on the news," he told Terri, "And I had this bottle in the fridge, and when I saw you, I knew what the right thing was to do with it." He handed it to her with a bouquet of flowers he'd picked up on the way.

Anna's pal, Jordyn, came up with her mom, Ellen. Ellen's partner, Jeanna, was still there from the night before, and Ellen came as soon as she'd made sure their older girl, Tori, was ready for school.

Tori and Jordyn are the same ages as our oldest two, and fast outdistancing their mothers in height. Jeanna and Ellen had been together eighteen years: Jeanna, a tiny and youthful woman who competes in triathlons for the almost fifty, Ellen, a red-haired, soothing-voiced woman from a large Mormon family.

The reporters and photographers were clearly fascinated by all these kids. Perhaps this wasn't what they'd expected when they got the tip that a line was forming, and marriage licenses were going to be granted that morning for lesbians and gays. Were they thinking drag queens and leather dykes, chanting members of ACT UP, college sweethearts, or gay septuagenarians who never thought they'd live to see the day? Graeme was photographed endlessly as he bobbed up and down, first in the backpack, and later in my arms. Reporters talked to each of the kids, always polite, never pushing, careful not to make the kids nervous, or hound them in any way.

It felt like the reporters on the spot were thrilled by this event. There was an unspoken sense they were cheerleaders, not just impartial observers of this social change happening with a bang, an interesting contrast to the television news anchors who looked serious, somber, and a little disapproving as they spoke to reporters on the scene from the safety of the newsroom, using words like "chaos," and "radical," and "revolutionary," as if they couldn't see that it was just couples queuing up quietly and civilly to get married.

The kids handled themselves well, talking to the reporters without fear, and with varying enthusiasm based on their shyer or more outgoing natures. All these children are growing up knowing their parents love one another, and they are well-practiced at being out about their families. None of us would have it any other way.

No Closet, After Kids

When we first had Duncan, I wanted to be such an exemplary mother that it wouldn't matter that I was also a lesbian. I was looking for some kind of benediction for daring to have him, simply because we selfishly wanted him. As if by being exemplary, I could be forgiven this audacious act, and he, and his siblings, would never feel the breath of prejudice.

I got over all that, some strange cocktail of internalized homophobia and post-partum depression that left me breathless.

Many years into lesbian motherhood, I can say from experience that there is a rule of reciprocity about being out. If you feel confident, and assume it will be fine, most often it is. Equally, if you approach revealing your sexual orientation as if it is a tender subject and potentially volatile, it will be.

During the long months we discussed becoming parents, before taking the plunge to make that happen, a major topic was being out. We knew that once we were parents, there was no going back.

The real transition from discreet to wide open was a little bumpy. We were the first out of the closet couple to have a baby at Providence Hospital in Seattle; yet, two months later, I was huddling inside our freezing nineteen-seventies Volkswagen van while Jannine brought Duncan to her office at Boeing to meet her co-workers, who knew that Jannine was adopting him (and wondered how she'd gotten her hands on a green-eyed, blonde, white baby in such a short time), but had still to learn that Jannine was living with the birth mother as well.

By the time he turned three months, and Jannine's co-parent adoption was finalized, her co-workers knew, and rose to the occasion.

At first, it felt like a big deal every time I had to say the words, "He doesn't have a dad, he has two moms." I would pause every time someone wanted to know what my husband did, or if he looked like his father, or how long I'd been married. Each time there was that subterranean fear. Would the mom next to me on the bench stand up and walk away? Would I hear a spirited lecture on modern morality? Would my child witness some kind of right-wing religious response right there in the line at the supermarket?

So far, no.

Jannine takes care of most of those "what does your husband do?" kind of questions by posting photographs of me and our kids in her cubicle at work, and she came out in the job interview when we moved to Portland, getting it on the table from day one.

I still get butterflies in my stomach when I'm meeting the parents of one of my kids' classmates for the first time while setting up a play date, or while assuring the parents (before their child comes over), that we have no guns, drugs, or weird relatives at our house. The butterflies aren't for me, but for our children. I worry that the friendship is going to be stalled by a parent who says, "No, Sarah can't play with Anna," when he or she discovers that Anna has two moms. Despite the butterflies, I have to be straightforward about who we are, so our kids will be, too.

Being straightforward can reap unexpected rewards. Years ago, a mom from our son's school turned to me and said, "So you stay home too, right? What does your husband do?"

I looked at her long bleached-blonde hair, serious cleavage, tight jeans, and high-heeled boots, knowing from previous conversations that she was from a large Catholic family, trying not to stereotype her any more than I'd want her to stereotype me.

Then I told her where "my partner" worked.

"Oh", she said. There was a long pause. Then she told me all about her two gay sisters, one of them struggling with it because of being Catholic. "She should just get over it and be happy." I still get reports from time to time on her sisters, one now expecting twins with her partner.

Because I was out, she felt free to talk about her sisters.

I think sometimes it is our children who will change the world for us. Three of our daughter's closest friends are from very traditional, Christian families, nice girls with good manners who like to come to our house because it's teeming with pets, and because, despite a culture that pressures girls to be mean, Anna is a nice girl. She has become expert at calmly explaining her family structure, knowing when to give details, and when to just give the basics, without apology, qualification, or hesitation. The only thing the girls have said about our family is how lucky Anna is to have two moms.

Duncan has been our biggest proponent from day one; his love and faith in us made it clear that we were OK the way we were, that we were the parents he wanted to have, and he has communicated that faith, whenever it has come up, for his entire thirteen years. He has a calm rationality that lent him the title "Mr. Switzerland" in second grade, and allows him to counter argument or prejudice without sinking to the level of his opposition. Graeme is entering a new world because of them.

I Have Wedding Issues Too

One persistent television reporter from Seattle wanted to interview Jannine, and me, live. He set us up in front of the lights, asked us to hold up our license application, and waited for his cue. Jannine hadn't slept all night. I was holding a squirming one year-old. When he got the signal that we were "go", he introduced us, then asked, "Why is it so important to be here today, right now, on the first day of legal same-sex marriage?"

Jannine answered. "For years now, Beren has wanted to get married, to have a wedding, and I was reluctant," she glanced at me, "But I told her if it ever became legal, I'd be one of the first in line."

And it hit me. My God, that was why she'd hustled right down to the County Building, to put her money where her mouth was. To let me know she hadn't just been whistling Dixie, or putting me off because, after all, hell would freeze over before she'd actually have to keep that promise. She meant it. We both had tears in our eyes.

Recently, marriage hadn't been a high priority. We were thrilled that legal advancements were a possibility, but it wasn't something I thought about with every waking breath.

There have been times though, when I couldn't say the same.

It would be a gross exaggeration to describe me as the happy-go-lucky type, though typically I am not one to loll around in misery by choice. However, years ago I entered a mire of matrimonial emotion, caused not only by Jannine's unwillingness to walk down the aisle, but by an assortment of unrelated circumstances: Duncan, who had dominated my landscape, entering first grade and spending half his waking hours with someone other than me; Anna spontaneously potty training herself in a day, starting preschool, and looking way too mature in her biking shorts and T-shirt; Jannine's having spent the entire summer obeying her company's unwritten rule that none of their employees should have a home life. We hardly saw her.

That September, I went away for a weekend by myself for the first time in seven years, and it had to be to a wedding.

I was happy that my cousin, Maddy, was getting married. She is an effervescent, generous soul who cannot help being drop-dead gorgeous, or that I feel like a piece of halibut in her presence. Her husband is swell, too. They've been fabulous to our kids, cheerleaders for us, and even managed to maintain their equilibrium when our Ford Escort station wagon was totaled in a four car pileup on the freeway, with them in it, one Thanksgiving afternoon. Despite any natural desire to avoid weddings in that kind of emotional condition, I *wanted* to go.

So did Jannine, but she stayed home with the kids because they were not at wedding compatible ages (they were yet to discover the joys of candle wax), and our budget was equally incompatible with four plane tickets plus hotel. Sadly, going solo robbed me of my identity, as well as my built-in conversation pieces: "This is Duncan, he'll be seven in November," "Anna just started preschool," and "Yes, they do look a lot alike, we cloned them in our basement." In close proximity to my family of origin, without Jannine and the kids as a buffer, I become not "Beren deMotier, partner, parent, and pundit wanna-be", I become "formerly-Laura, dysfunctional family member, and eternally inadequate younger sibling." It's not a pretty sight.

Despite that, it was a good time. Partly because my friend Laurie lent me a killer brick red cocktail dress (since then, I only wear Laurie's clothes to weddings), partly because, despite being held in a vast, decaying, gothic castle plopped down in the middle of Los Angeles, the wedding party, and those attending, were not a prim and proper group; even the elderly relatives from Turkey were ready to party. It may be the first wedding where the hora was followed by *YMCA* on the dance floor. I think it was the sense of communal joy that spurred me to skip making inspired orations on gay and lesbian marriage to anyone who would listen, and to sink later to a depth of depression that had Jannine scooping me from the floor with a spatula.

Certainly being premenstrual at the time added to my poor, poor, pitiful me outlook, as well as the impending onset of a cold, but I can't be the only lesbian who's become unbalanced around weddings. At times, I've wished I were one of those lesbians who is comfortable with nonconformity, the kind who sports a nose ring, a crew cut, and facial hair, impervious to the pressures of society at large and living by her own rules (or the rules of her chosen subculture). But, alas, I'm embarrassingly mainstream. We're born into a society that feeds us expectations, potentials, and judgments about everything, and whether I swallow them whole, throw up the whole mess, go hungry, or selectively binge on them at irregular intervals, they're part of who I am.

For me, weddings did what a good therapist couldn't do in twenty sessions: bring to the surface a whole lot of suppressed sorrow. Not about my lifestyle, which is just fine, thank you very much, has the usual ups and downs, and is about as unthreatening as a cup of organic yogurt, but in the way it is, or has been, treated by the ones I love.

And I'm one of the lucky ones; I haven't been disowned, disavowed, or sent to shock therapy. Yet, was I wrong to mourn that Jannine and I could never have the kind of wedding I witnessed, one where both families were enthusiastic, willing to work through differences, and just happy that the couple had found each other? Without spending fifteen years getting used to the idea?

I know that for many gays, marriage seems as assimilation-ist and atavistic as becoming a Freemason or joining the PTA, but even for them, it must hurt to know that we are expected, by many in this country, to be happy our relationships are "tolerated," as if that is all we should hope for. The dictionary defines tolerate as "to endure without repugnance; to put up with." We deserve better than that.

I also know that, as a community, we have other fish to fry. We have adoption rights, health care issues, legal discrimination, and oh, our nation being bogged down in a military quagmire in Iraq. Marriage seems a luxury when gay people are dying from beatings and lack of adequate medical care. Most of us would be happy to get a date that turned out well, much less an engagement ring. But just call me a glutton, a Bruce Bawer "place at the table" kind of girl because I want the luxury of legal marriage, even if just for that piece of paper that proves our relationship is something more than tolerated.

I Come From Interesting Stock

Multnomah County Council members Lisa Naito, Maria Rojo de Steffey, and Serena Cruz came by to congratulate several of the waiting couples on their way into the building. Press photographers were snapping images that would fuel the fire of dissent about the commissioners' decision to issue marriage licenses to same-sex couples, eventually leading to an unsuccessful recall attempt for two of the county commissioners, and a public apology from County Chair Diane Linn, not for offering the licenses to same-sex couples, she doesn't apologize for that, but for the way she went about it.

These four women who voted to legally recognize our relationships risked political suicide by agreeing that the Oregon State Constitution required equal privileges and immunities to all, and by listening to the legal opinion of County Attorney Agnes Sowle, who said that those privileges and immunities included marriage. Sowle also suggested that the Multnomah County Commission could be vulnerable to lawsuits if they didn't allow same-sex marriage. The Commissioners, with the exception of Lonnie Roberts, who opposes same-sex marriage (but supports civil unions), and was left out of the loop (thus the apology by Diane Linn), voted to act immediately, to keep same-sex marriage from sinking under the mire of public debate, while the opposition mobilized, filing petition after petition to make darn sure same-sex marriage in Multnomah County never came to pass.

While I am sure in my mind that these four intelligent, politically savvy women were only interpreting the state constitution as accurately as they could, my heart prefers a more imaginative scenario: all four commissioners, two blondes and two brunettes with a heavy load of responsibility, were letting their hair down at a Hawthorne area brew pub after a tough day in politics, their high heels kicked off under their stools, their symbolic neckties loosened, surrounded by denizens of the district in organically grown recycled cotton, second hand black leather, and brand new Birkenstocks, when one of them took a long drink of microbrew, and said, "If I have to sit through one more all-day meeting, I am going to scream." "Yeah, me too," agreed the commissioner on the next stool. Beside her, the third commissioner muttered, "You know what, if I could do one thing before my term is over, it would be to legalize same-sex marriage." The fourth commissioner slapped her hand on the bar and said, "Me, too. I never get to do enough to make people happy, I'm always putting out fires." "You know, there is a legal precedent here," added the first woman. "Yeah, we'd be heroines if we could make it happen," the second woman said, "To some of the voters anyway." "We'd never live it down," number four suggested. "And we might never work in government again," the third one added, "But we'd make a lot of families happy." I imagine them all silent a moment, drinking in the consequences, then looking at each other and saying, "Let's do it."

Lisa finally arrived with Katie and Jacob, her long dark hair loose and wet from the shower. She was flustered and beaming, carrying folding chairs for which there was now no room, her eyes bright with disbelief and barely contained joy. Katie and Jacob joined the other children: Katie to link arms with Anna, Jacob to enter into a serious discussion of D & D with Duncan.

Soon, Tom Disrud, the Associate Minister of the First Unitarian Church, arrived in support of his many parishioners at the front of the line. He was greeted with cheers. Tom is a shy, brotherly man, and openly gay. His sermons meander over everyday issues, bringing meaning to mundane details; he seems human, not an authoritarian god-like person who will tell us what to believe, or how to be a good Unitarian, as if anyone could agree on that. When he speaks, you can imagine him puttering in his garden, wondering if his rhododendron is dying or dormant, pondering how to fertilize the grass without harming the environment, or whether he should keep his lawn Portland-style and let it die in the summer and rise again in the fall, surely the most Judeo-Christian of lawn managements.

Tom joined us for the duration, ducking into the building to check out whether he could marry us there and then, at the County Building, when we got our licenses. He came back to let us know he was asked to refrain from marrying couples inside the building, in consideration of the crush, but he was willing to make the sidewalk a sacred space if that was what we desired.

I tried again to reach my mother on the phone. I'd tried twice before with no answer, worrying since she is generally up by five. Then, she answered with a tentative, "Hello?"

"Hi, it's me. We're in line at the County Building, and we're getting a marriage license."

"What!?" she screamed.

"I know, I know. Turn on the news! We don't know if we're getting married today because there may be a waiting period; if there is, we're getting married

Saturday, if not, today." She squealed so loudly that Terri could hear her a few feet away.

"Do you want to be there if we get married today?"

She yelled, "Do I want to be there? Of course I want to be there! I've waited my whole life for this," adding, "And I'm going to throw a reception and by golly, the relatives are all going to come!"

I was unbelievably happy, this reaction was better than I could have hoped for. She was happy for me. She got it. She wanted to be there. I told her I'd let her know when I knew what was going to happen. We hung up and I was smiling, Chris and Terri hugged me, happy that this went so very well.

My family of origin has offered challenges over the years, and to be fair, I have offered them in return. My mother and I have the usual mother/daughter conflict, but we also have multigenerational junk between us. I come from interesting stock. I am one of two sisters, born of the eldest of three sisters, born of the eldest of three sisters, born of an only daughter. Luckily, I am a younger daughter, so I was able to have two sons without messing up the whole "girls only" tradition that runs along the elder daughter line, though my sister has so far failed to fulfill her quota.

The women in our family also tend to graduate from high school early (and have been college educated for generations), heading off to college at seventeen. I got my braces off the day before leaving for college, and turned seventeen only days before, which, in retrospect, didn't help my transition to higher education, though it did attract large numbers of leftist young men who wanted to sleep with girls the same age as their younger sisters.

Our women have also tended to choose difficult men. My father was a moody, alcoholic, folk musician/early computer geek who drank himself to death; my mother's father, a successful writer, loved my grandmother passionately, yet they engaged in legendary, alcohol-fueled fights during cocktail parties that had the guests running for the door; my great grandfather stuck his head in the gas oven after the stock market crashed in 1929, and my great, great grandfather ran off with his secretary, leaving his wife (known in the family as The Victorian Beauty) in the lurch and on the hands of her grown daughter, the widow of the man who stuck his head in the gas oven. As if she didn't have enough problems.

One might think all this had something to do with my lack of interest in mating for life with a man, but really, I was born this way. From an early age, it was plain to me that women were prettier than men, we spoke the same language (that whole Mars/Venus thing never worked for me), and if I couldn't grow up and marry my zaftig, red-headed school crush, Tina (who I followed around like a faithful dog during my years at Maple Elementary in Campbell River), I wouldn't marry at all.

Not that I didn't give boys a try. I had a busy three years of heterosexual activity from sixteen to nineteen, including nearly year-long relationships with: 1. an asthmatic, drug-addled electric guitarist with a great profile who taught me Human Sexuality 400 in his basement bedroom, loved me so much that he threatened to kill me with a straight razor, and while able to spout intelligent, feminist analysis one moment, was a raving anger management problem the next. It was while the straight razor was held against my throat, and he started muttering about his grandfather's gun, that I thought, "I could die here," and decided to do a geographic to college, instead of enrolling locally. 2. A nice guy who happened to be the Resident Advisor at my freshman dorm. He was a handsome, wholesome, strapping specimen who sat down next to me on the dorm steps a couple days after classes began, to ask how I was adjusting to campus life, and never knew what hit him. I suspect that I scared him to death in my red polyvinyl cowboy boots, a seventeen year-old nymphet with a graduate degree in sex who was willing to home tutor, and having found someone decent (yet warped, I discovered, in a good way), wanted nothing but him, him, him ... except, perhaps, that lovely young lady in drama class? 3. A self-described "thief" from Buffalo with a crooked moral compass. He was cute, smooth, and probably about as faithful as your average Hollywood husband, though I was every bit as bad. I broke up with him by telling him I was involved with a girl he'd dated, a blonde beauty I met when I was sixteen and she, fourteen. She'd skipped down the smoking area at Lincoln High School in Seattle, her long, golden hair, sparkling blue eyes, and rosy cheeks a vision, and I'd turned to the girl next to me and said, "Who is that?"

The girl looked at me like I was nuts, "She's your boyfriend's little sister!"

But it wasn't the golden girl who actually wrenched the door of my closet wide; it was athletic, suave, gender-bending Jennifer from my Women in Literature class who managed that, though she might have mentioned she had a live-in lover before she stole my heart.

Ironically, she went on to date the golden girl ...

I gave dating boys the old college try, mostly for my mother. She wanted me to be heterosexual in a big way, having sat me down when I was fifteen and informed me that sex was the center of the universe (a confusing message), and I gave it my dysfunctional best. When I came out to her twenty-one years ago, eager to tell her about the flawless Jen-Jen, she insisted that she had "two straight daughters," and she'd have "two straight son-in-laws."

But, now she was so happy I was marrying a nice girl, instead. And she wanted to be there.

Why Don't You
Marry Your Dog?

"Repent!"

"God hates this!"

"You are an abomination to God!"

"How dare you bring children to this place of sin?"

Around eight o'clock, two protesters came to rain on our parade. Both of them were youngish men, Caucasian, and brown haired. One of them wore a white shirt and tie, and just carried a big sign reading "Repent Perverts," at first standing across the street, then standing in the street, and then finally standing so close he could almost touch the couples in line, as if his fear of the enemy had diminished over time. The other man, a muscle-bound fanatic, spewed biblical hate-speak at a fevered pitch, like an auctioneer for God, selling our souls to hell. He never seemed to draw breath as he shrieked his vitriolic distaste for our desire to marry, at one point while holding up a sign that read, "Can you escape the wrath of God?"

His message was falling flat in our section, since we're the sort of women with bumper stickers like "my God is too big to fit in any one religion," "co-exist," and "sorry I missed church, I was busy practicing witchcraft and becoming a lesbian," despite being regular church attendees.

He began screaming, "Why don't you marry your dog?" over and over again, as if to pound home his point that gay men and lesbians were not only an abomination, but mere animals, no more worthy of love and marriage than household pets. The noise of the jubilant crowd couldn't drown him out, and our son Duncan didn't miss a word.

Duncan is famous for his hearing. We can whisper three rooms away, yet he hears all, occasionally shouting interjections into the conversation we were trying to keep private. He is a challenge at holiday time.

This talent didn't help him that morning. It was when the man was screaming, "Why don't you marry your dog?" that I saw Duncan curled up under a blanket on one of the lawn chairs, his hands over his ears, his eyes shut, and my heart went cold. It is one thing to know in your head that there are people who don't support your family, it is quite another to hear your parents called an abomination and their torturous stint in hell described at leisure.

I wanted our children with us, but, being one of those individuals who always imagine the worst, in Technicolor, I had feared what could happen. I'd asked Lisa the night before, as we watched our spouses on the news, "Will the kids be safe? Will there be a lot of protesters? Do you think they'll throw things at us?" Lisa had been confident. "Right," she said, "There will be a handful of them, and hundreds of us. I don't think so," her unspoken words painting a picture of hordes of happy couples attacking anyone who dared hurt our children. She was right, but even if no one threw stones, the words still hurt.

Not that we haven't been hurt before.

It was five years ago now that a thirteen year-old boy asked Chris and me, "Does it hurt?" when Chris and I were doing a speaking engagement at Oregon Episcopal School. We'd been invited by our neighbor, Bonnie, who teaches middle school there, and thought that since the kids were studying anti-gay legislation as part of social studies, they should hear from honest-to-God gay people themselves on the subject.

Measure 9 was coming up on the November ballot, and we were there to talk about how it would eradicate gay people from public education: in history, in literature, in health class, in efforts to end harassment among students. The measure read: "Sexual orientation, as it relates to homosexuality and bisexuality, is a divisive subject matter not necessary to the instruction of students in public schools. Notwithstanding any other law or rule, the instruction of behaviors relating to homosexuality and bisexuality shall not be presented in a public school in a manner which encourages, promotes or sanctions such behaviors." The obvious result of Measure 9 would be that negative things could be said about bisexuality or homosexuality, but to oppose those statements would mean sanctions against the school. Teachers would be silenced from saying anything to defend us, or our kids. We would be taboo.

It was inspirational talking with those intelligent, thoughtful kids; they asked good questions.

Questions like: "Is there anything about the measure that you agree with?" "Would the measure affect just what teachers say and do, or would speech between students be affected?" "Would you be able to talk to us like this, if the measure passed?"

Toward the end, they asked a few more personal questions: "How did your families react when you came out?" "How do your children feel about your being gay, do they think it's cool?"

And right at the end, "Does it hurt?"

We had an answer for that one. Chris and I had talked about it that morning. We both agreed that even in a life full of friends and kids and spouses, it hurt like hell to have to fight continually for our dignity and equality.

It's hard to get used to being demonized.

Chris explained to the OES students the basic difference of opinion between those for, and those against Measure 9, that those who support the Measure believe that being gay is a choice, that it is a moral and ethical failing that brings joy to no one. We, she went on, speaking for those against Measure 9, believe that being gay is natural and normal, like being left-handed or blonde. This, she explained, is why it is almost impossible to bridge this division.

Measure 9 failed, by a tiny margin, thanks to a lot of volunteers going door to door. But I was chicken; I couldn't bring myself to canvass against the Measure. I couldn't face hearing, straight from the voter's mouth, that he or she thought that I was a "divisive issue" and "unnecessary to the public instruction of students," that my life and I were not things to be "encouraged, promoted or sanctioned" in any way.

Yes, Chris told the boy, it is painful for anyone to think our lives are so unworthy.

Goin' to the Chapel and
We're Gonna Get Married

Duncan was quickly reassured, and assured us that it wasn't that he was scared, or had doubts about our marrying that day, he just found the protesters incomprehensible. He couldn't wrap his mind around their point of view; how could they believe as they did when the evidence was right in front of them that we were good people, that we only wanted to get married, just like anyone else?

Now the parents were worried. The words "San Diego" went through my mind, as the memory of a tear gas bomb thrown into the family section at a Pride Parade in San Diego years before made me even more aware of how vulnerable we were. The other moms took a moment to check in with their kids, assuring them they were safe and among friends, even if those guys with signs were telling us to go to hell. Jacob blew off the protesters with ease, calling them idiots, and the girls seemed to find it easier to block out the words than Duncan, telling us all they heard was noise.

We all knew it was time to rein in the kids, who had been using all their pent up energy, and all those donuts, by bursting into the only open space in front of the County Building entry, where the reporters were standing (when they weren't moving out of the way of a leaping child). But now, too many strangers were passing through, it was time to keep them close, in case a silent protester was moving amid the crowd, waiting to do mischief.

Just when we'd gathered the kids, a woman brought noise-makers. She handed them out to the kids, telling them, "Drown those guys out!" This delighted the kids and stressed the adults, who, while jubilant, celebratory, and glad the kids were entertained, were still human beings with eardrums they were fond of. Graeme was not sure what he thought about all the shrill noise, but when Jacob gave him a noisemaker to hold, he was quite content, and gnawed it like a happy beaver.

Near nine o'clock, the people in line behind us became impatient and began pushing forward, while Sheriffs pushed us politely back, to clear the now-opened doors to the building, so that we were compactly sandwiched between the people behind and the traffic heading in and out of the building, like lesbian sardines and their small fry.

Most of the men and women entering the County Building were smiling as they snaked around us, weaving through reporters, supporters, and law enforcement. A few had the harassed look of someone who'd had to park blocks away wearing uncomfortable shoes, with no warning that any of this was going on, somehow missing the news on radio, television, or on the front page of the paper.

Even as the news conference about the decision to issue marriage licenses to same-sex couples began inside the building at 9:00, we wondered if it would really happen, or if at the last moment, something would happen to snatch the possibility of marriage away: an injunction, a court order, a phone call from the Governor, a sudden loss of nerve by the County Commissioners who were risking so much for our right to marry. County sheriffs were becoming numerous on the steps of the building, keeping back the protesters, keeping the doors clear, and the media in line.

Graeme was getting restless. He'd been up for hours, and still wasn't getting any "nummies," our word for nursing. He didn't know what the heck was going on, and looked around as if thinking, "This is not my beautiful house. This is not my beautiful bed. Who are all these people, and why are they so loud?" He'd been bounced in the backpack, photographed endlessly, and was stiff with layers to protect him from the forty-two degree weather. He was struggling in my arms like a salmon dying to get upstream, so Jannine suggested I take him into the lobby—surely the county officials would understand the needs of a toddler?

While Jannine saw this as a solution, I saw this as a potential problem. If you allow one child some freedom, they'll all want it. Reluctantly, I took him into the lobby. Anna asked to come. Duncan appeared with his D & D book. Katie slipped in to be with Anna. McKenzie and Jordyn followed, Ellen along as well, to look for a form to fill out. Jacob completed the mob, and Graeme had hardly enough room to breathe.

Our forms were filled out, and held tightly in Jannine's hand as she gathered our things together in anticipation. We'd carefully filled out our license application, double-checking for accuracy, perplexed that both "bride" and "groom" sections had boxes to check indicating gender. Were these always there? Jannine had grabbed a form from the lobby, requesting the normal three-day waiting period before marriage be waived, when the door was opened at nine.

On our waiver application, under "reason for request" we wrote a long-winded explanation that boiled down to: since our kids were already out of school to share the wait in line, we wanted to get married the same day, so they wouldn't miss any additional school. We hoped it had a nice responsible parent ring to it, when really we just didn't want to miss the chance to marry.

Finally, it was time. We kept our kids close, swept Graeme up into my arms, and waded into the crowded building, a picture of happiness and hope that ended up on *The News Hour with Jim Lehrer* later that day. In Sunnyside, Washington, neighboring town to now infamous "Mad Cow" Mabton, Jannine's grandfather saw us on his television, and called our home to tell us we were celebrities, and that maybe we could "give him a call" to let him know what was up in Portland. In Yakima, Jannine's aunts and cousins had already heard about our imminent nuptials because Aunt Bunny got a call from her friend, Karen, saying she'd heard Jannine on the radio being interviewed. The news spread through the Eastern Washington grapevine and our e-mail in-baskets started to fill with copies of news clippings sent by supportive family.

Once in the building, our forms were checked for accuracy by *Basic Rights Oregon* volunteers who made sure we hadn't altered any of the wording on the form, then we were escorted by a sheriff past the collected media to a county official, who told us where to stand in line for our license.

By then, we knew that two other couples had been issued licenses at the news conference: two professional, clean cut "poster couples," one male, one female, chosen in advance by BRO, and offered up to the public as sacrificial lambs for same-sex marriage, to be pictured in every paper, Web site, and television news story for weeks to come. They didn't have to wait in line all night, shivering inside layers of coats, scarves, and winter boots, and had relatives and friends on hand (which we all would have loved), but then again, we had an experience they didn't get to have. There was a lot of love, support, celebration, and sense of community in that line. We were all so glad to be getting married at last.

Inside the licensing office, Bonnie Tinker and her partner, Sara, were given an enormous bouquet sent for the first couple to receive a license, the bicycle delivery man apparently unaware that two other couples already had licenses (or did the sender specify where to deliver them?), and were hustling out, we presumed, to get married that moment.

We were next, our dearest friends behind us, beaming support. The woman at the counter was helpful, smiling, and a little nervous; this was new to her, too. All the county employees seemed keyed up, but happy, as if everyone knew that this was a momentous occasion. Our clerk explained how we paid at the next window, and how the person officiating the marriage, the judge or minister, would sign and send in the form, where it would be put on the county record and *that* is what would make us married. She made sure we understood all the hoops we needed to jump through to make it legal. She showed us the frame-worthy symbolic license and the personalized congratulatory certificate from Diane Linn, the Chair of the Multnomah County Council, both now framed on our wall.

The clerk didn't show us the family planning materials included, thinking we didn't need them, though I occasionally joke that I am the only lesbian in history who needs to have her tubes tied, so easily do I become pregnant, and how willing I am to do so, given the chance.

Hardly believing it was true, that we held a marriage license in our hands, we went to the payment window, stopping just long enough to answer a European reporter who asked us how long we'd been together, the universal first question on this day of commitment. The clerk at this window took our sixty dollars cash, smiled, stamped us "paid," and gave us our license back with congratulations. We held up the license; there were cheers and clapping. Terri shouted, "So you finally made an honest woman out of her!" to Jannine. We lingered a little, hoping to watch our friends get their licenses, but were urged toward the door by county officials, to keep the traffic flowing. Before we left the building, we saw Tom again, and said, "Marry us Tom!" "Gladly," he replied, arranging to meet us and any of our friends and fellow Unitarians at the church by ten-thirty, if we could wait that long. License in hand, we could.

DOMA is Apparently Not Enough

It was hard knowing that while we were celebrating our seventeen year union by getting married, our president was trying to amend the constitution of the United States to make darned sure that we couldn't get married all over the country, and that if Multnomah County, or San Francisco, or Massachusetts let us do it, it would be federally non-existent.

It seems like yesterday that our last president, an ironic proponent of the sanctity of marriage considering his predilection for adultery in the Oval Office, voted to pass the Defense of Marriage Act. Whether he earnestly believed that heterosexual couples were the chosen people, or he was so convinced by pollsters that the average American wasn't ready for us to get hitched, he turned on the gay constituency he pledged to support, leaving us disappointed, but knowing he was by far the lesser of two evils.

With DOMA, I was bewildered at the lightning-fast reaction to the threat of same-sex marriage, when Hawaii dared to question whether it had a right to discriminate, and if it would pay to become the gay marriage capital of the world. States scrambled to outlaw same-sex marriage, should it try to invade their borders. And now President Bush was trying to nix that possibility for the entire nation. That this issue should mobilize people like nothing this side of nuclear war or an outbreak of Mad Cow Disease was not only shocking, it tells it like it is.

Because this is it, isn't it? The last bastion was being scaled. Are we members of society and therefore guaranteed life, liberty, and the pursuit of happiness including marriage to the one we love (or like, lust after, don't want to lose, looks good at the time, or has cool appliances, just like the rest of the population), or are we indeed perverts and beyond the pale?

I forget that to some people, we're still these frightening Things that are after their children, to molest them, or steal them, or convert them; these individuals missing somehow that we've spent the last two decades becoming role models for intentional parenthood: coaching Little League, joining the PTA, fundraising for public schools, and spending megabucks at Toys-R-Us. I still see letters to the

editor that read, "If we give the homosexuals marriage, they'll want to have children next!" as if we haven't been doing so in large numbers for years, and quite
successfully according to repeated studies which indicate no discernible difference
emotionally or intellectually between children raised by gay parents, and those
raised by straights, except that the kids raised by gay parents tend to be more
open minded about "alternative lifestyles."

Some things have changed though since DOMA passed in 1996. The "sicko
stew" the right wing cooked up for public consumption back then, that tossed us
everyday gays (mowing our lawns, shopping at Costco, or driving a Subaru when
we're not watching *Queer as Folk, The L-Word,* or *Sesame Street*) in with the child
molesters, the rapists, the pornographers, and, say, the Jeffrey Dahmers of the
world, isn't being served up as the main course this time. We have a compassion-
ate, conservative opposition that doesn't want to throw us in jail or conversion
therapy; they just want to "preserve the sanctity of marriage" for God's Chosen
People.

While there are plenty of enlightened heterosexual souls out there who really
do think we're human beings, same as them, or are willing to vote as if they do,
most still draw the line at marriage. Some cite centuries-old tradition (ignoring
that marriage traditions vary the world over, and over time), some can't get over
the "who's gonna wear the dress?" dilemma, and many feel that, "You can keep
your jobs, keep your homes, maybe even keep your kids, but gay marriage is *going
too far!*"

Gays themselves continue to be split on the issue. Even as we hurried off with
our licenses, there were gay men and lesbians fretting in front of their televisions
that this was going to set the movement back ten years, and was no part of the
modern gay lifestyle anyway. It shocks me how many in our community don't
want us to push for the right to marry or are actually opposed to same-sex marriage.

No one is forcing them to marry.

The "marriage isn't part of the gay lifestyle, it's so bourgeois" argument may
sound like Queer cutting-edge radicalism, but I suspect it's a by-product of all
that sicko stew we've been force-fed over the years. It's hard to accept yourself as
a worthy member of Society (with a capital S) on a steady diet of "sicko," "fag-
got," and "I wish you were dead." It takes a toll. Sure, maybe some of us are
above plebian concerns like marriage and monogamy, and have developed a more
modern mode of living and celebrating love. Some of us may be counter-culture
neo-pagans, and that's why we're tattooed to the nines and refuse to buy into the

establishment. But then again, we may think "normal" was not an option we ever had.

Marriage equals "normal"; the recognition that we are equal in heart, and that's why our president is fighting against it so hard, to keep the fact that we, the people, of the United States of America, are gay and straight and lesbian and bi and those definitions are about the love between consenting adults. When we fall in love, we feel just the same, make the same commitment, and deserve the same rights and responsibilities. How can there be any question?

Running the Gauntlet

We pushed open the glass doors of the Multnomah County Building, and some-one shouted, "Show us your license!" We held it up and thunderous applause broke out from the hundreds of people there: waiting couples, supportive friends, journalists who couldn't help themselves and a wave of understanding and love washed over us.

We were still in shock that this had really happened, a Bambi-in-the-head-lights response to a miracle. A reporter stuck a microphone in our faces and asked, "How does it feel to have your license? Are you going off to get married?" as we were ushered by sheriffs to a clear space further down, where the muscular protester latched onto us, screaming so close we could feel his breath. Jannine and I ignored him, answered a couple of questions, then saw some of our friends emerge from the building, and cheered for them as they held their licenses up, Terri holding Marty's hand in triumph, Chris grinning from ear to ear and already crying. The young lesbian with multi-colored hair who'd cheered us on through the morning came up to us and thanked us. "You are my inspiration! And I'm not even getting married," she told us, "I don't even have a girlfriend!"

We joined up with Marty and Terri, and Chris and Lisa to coordinate rides back home and to the Unitarian church. Our belongings were spread throughout our herd of vehicles: sleeping bags in one, port-a-potty in another, food, drink, and clothing scattered here and there.

As we broke through the crowd to the sidewalk, we were joined by a retinue of three who paced us step-by-step in a closely formed huddle: a reporter, a strong, silent Multnomah County sheriff, and the screaming protester. The sheriff said nothing, but the reporter walked backward in front of us for the entire block, tell-ing the kids, "He doesn't know what he's talking about. Don't listen to him. Your family is great. He's an idiot …" because the protester was shrieking at us full volume, focusing on the children as he spewed, "How dare you bring these children to this filth? How dare you bring them to this place of sin? You are an abomination to God. God hates this, God hates this, God hates this!" The girls didn't acknowledge his presence, instead they loudly planned a counter protest to tell the world how wonderful this day was, and Duncan looked steadily ahead, eager to be out of contact with this fanatic, whose spit was flying with his words. I covered Graeme's ears to lessen the din, and didn't make eye contact with him, a man who thought he was protecting children when really he was scaring them and giving good Christians a bad name.

At the corner, the protester turned back, the sheriff following him, and the reporter gave us a thumb's up as we made our way to our cars, shaken.

Four of the kids and I hopped into Marty's minivan, Terri and Jannine in ours, while Chris and Lisa climbed into our little Honda with their kids to drive it back to their house and pick up their own Sienna minivan. The streets were filling up with news vans from Seattle, and cars were parked bumper to bumper for streets, as gay men and lesbians queued up on three sides of the city block in their eagerness to legally commit. Terri ended up running back to say hello to friends, avoiding the protesters by going the long way past the hundreds of waiting couples. She told Jannine it was like being a celebrity at the Academy Awards; she'd forgotten to leave the marriage license in the van, it was still in her hand, and couples cheered as she passed, asked her questions, shouted congratulations, and smiled from ear to ear.

By the end of the day, over four hundred couples received licenses and Multnomah County made twenty-five thousand dollars. The highest number of licenses on any previous day was sixty.

As Marty started up the van, the protesters were already forgotten. We were excited beyond belief, incredulous that after waiting so long, it had happened so fast.

I really needed another Diet Coke.

Just For the Taste of It

There's a great running gag in the movie *Airplane*. Lloyd Bridges plays this seasoned pilot in the control tower talking down a shell shocked veteran who's taken over flying the plane when the pilots are stricken with food poisoning. The Bridges character keeps saying, "I guess I picked a bad week to give up smoking," as he lights up a cigarette, then "I picked a bad week to give up drinking," as he downs a double bourbon, then "I picked a bad week to give up snorting coke," "I picked a bad week to give up sniffing glue …" as things go from bad to worse.

That's what I've felt like from time to time, though it wasn't smoking, drinking, or sniffing glue which was issuing the siren call.

It was Diet Coke.

Innocuous stuff or death trap; despite my decades-long dependency, I suspect the latter. I'm not exactly main-lining it, it's more like a can here, a bottle there, the summer glory of a Big Gulp. But believing as I do, logic dictates that I would never again imbibe that dark, bubbly, and potentially noxious elixir.

Ha.

There are worse things to be addicted to, right? Actually, my Diet Coke addiction is one of those surrogate addictions you see in action at any AA meeting when the coffee and cigarettes flow. Not only does it keep me off the well-worn alcoholic path bred deep in my DNA, it was also my dietary crutch for eons.

To the teenage girl who could never match her mother's twenty-three inch waist, a drink like Diet Coke (or in the olden days Tab) seemed like a godsend. Who needed food when you had a Diet Coke? You got the sensory pleasure of sucking on a bottle or straw, you got the caffeine buzz and the strange woozy feeling of the Nutra-sweet rearranging your gene pool. You got a slightly nauseating feeling of fullness if you drank enough, which warded off those inconvenient urges to eat.

These days, I'm more moderate, as if I had a choice. One of the nice things about having babies is that you have an excuse to put on a pound or two. There *are* moms out there with cutting board abs, but unless you want to give up your life to exercise (see "Demi Moore"), you've got to relax, because those stretch marks and Shar Pei belly are here to stay.

I've been Diet Coke-free before, like during my first pregnancy. I was good: oatmeal, V8 juice, and cream cheese and cucumber sandwiches on whole wheat. No sugary snacks, no junk food, no soda. I must have complained more than I realized though, because immediately after the labor from hell, the receptionist from our doctor's office (who'd witnessed the labor from hell) placed an ice cold can in my hand, patted my arm, and said, "You deserve it."

A couple of years ago, Jannine and I made a concerted effort to quit soda, mostly because it was such a nasty habit to pass along to the children. Unlike, say, smoking, it's not the end of the world, but it's still not good. I don't think I lasted a week.

We have all these idealistic desires as parents. My wife and I would like to be the kind of people who buy organic produce, free-range chicken, and grow a half-acre garden out back. We'd like to be naturopathic, chemical-free individuals raising children without pesticides in their veins and cartoon characters in their brains.

Alas, we can't even take our vitamins on a regular basis, though we did give up beef, and we're working on the free-range thing. Our kids don't have every kid's meal toy invented, just half. The sick thing is that every time we find ourselves in fast food heaven, my paranoid theory that not only Diet Coke, but *all* fast food is laced with addictive chemicals is only reinforced. Yet, I still yearn to drink the stuff.

One time, when the kids were younger, I decided to get that cola monkey off my back, cold turkey.

I couldn't have picked a worse time. My urge to come clean fell just as Jannine was embarking on a business trip for a week. While she was away in sunny California, I endured colds, flus, and school crises, plus the rigors of housebreaking a brand-new (and increasingly humongous) puppy. Though I wasn't exactly talking any jet planes down from the sky, I was talking myself blue in the face trying to persuade our two year-old that pushing the puppy's head down would probably result in reconstructive surgery, for her. I was hearing that siren call in a big way. By the time I rolled into the airport to pick up Jannine (Anna puking in her car seat in the back), there was nothing left to do but laugh.

And go get a Diet Coke.

"Don't Do Anything
Until I Get There!"

We caravanned past the line of waiting couples, honking our support, looking like a new ad for the Toyota Sienna in *The Advocate*. As we drove by, Marty suddenly squawked, "The chairs!" realizing we'd left a pile of lawn chairs stacked by the County Building doors. She shook her head, "We'll just have to get them later." It wasn't a time to worry about trifles like lawn chairs.

Marty phoned her mother and her friend, Ann, to meet her at the church. Marty's mom told her, "Don't do anything until I get there!" She'd waited a long time to see this day. As a minister's wife, she'd been to a ton of weddings. This was her turn to be the mother of the bride.

I borrowed Marty's phone and called my mother. She answered on the first ring. "If you want to be there, come now," I told her. She lived just across the Columbia River in Vancouver, so this was possible. She got the address of the church, confirmed directions, and said she'd get there as soon as she could.

In the other van, Jannine was wishing she'd called her parents at five in the morning and asked them to come down. But she also knew that with her father's recent health problems (that blood clot passing through his heart), he shouldn't be hopping in the car for a three hour drive. She'd spoken to them earlier, and had their blessing. She called her good friend, Liz, who works downtown (and would later marry her longtime love, Nan), who said she'd be there, pronto.

None of us hesitated about getting married as soon as possible. None of us wanted to live with the sorrow of knowing we could have been married if we'd done it right away, before the courts stopped it. While we would love to have gathered friends, chosen outfits, and flown relatives in, we knew that we might not have the time. This gift was ephemeral, and it was important to get married, to mark our long time as couples, and not let that opportunity slip away.

It was also important to send the message that we really want this. We are ready, willing, and able to take on the responsibilities and rights of marriage. We've had the responsibilities already in our long, but unrecognized marriages, now we'd like to receive some of the rights: the legal ones.

The $600 Date

Jannine and I blew $600 one day a couple years ago, to purchase as many of the legal protections that come free of charge with marriage as the law allows. We agreed, during an emotionally charged latte break afterwards, that we'd rather have been spending the dollars on a weekend for two in San Francisco, with the attendant romantic mileage you can get from that kind of investment (ka-ching, deposit into the emotional bank account). But, we are responsible spouses and mothers, so we went to our lawyer and blew our wad there.

It all started when Jannine was experiencing a rare case of don't-want-to-go-to-work-itis. She'd been putting in long hours and enough was enough. Since it's much more fun to play hooky with someone else, than to hooky alone, she talked me into blowing off my plans, and we had a gay film fest in the privacy of our basement while the children were safe at school.

Not a panting porn gay film fest (I'm notoriously porn-averse), but our own little two-fer: one mild, *What Makes a Family*, taped off cable for us by a friend, and one wild, *Bound* on DVD, which while not porn, is definitely salacious and fun. Gina Gershon is welcome in my basement any day.

It wasn't Gina and her lawless biceps that had us scuttling off to a lawyer, though. It was *What Makes a Family*, a Lifetime Network movie starring Brooke Shields and Cherry Jones. It's based on the true story of two women who fell in love, had a commitment ceremony, bore a child by artificial insemination, only to discover the biological mother has systemic lupus. When she dies, leaving the other mother without legal protection, the grandparents sweep in and take the child away.

While the story ends well after a tear-jerking plot line (there was a wad of used tissues by my feet), and Brooke is reunited with their daughter, it was a cautionary tale of why wills and powers-of-attorney are too important to delay.

We were both shaken when the movie was over, and even *Bound* couldn't restore our equilibrium. We knew we needed to revisit the documents we'd made nine years before, when I was pregnant with our first child. They far from spelled out our current intentions.

Unlike the characters in the movie, who lived in Florida where same-sex adoption is still illegal, we are both the legal parents of our children. So, our lawyer assured us, the situation that occurred in the movie was virtually impossible. Virtually, he said. Sadly, there is always that shadow of a doubt based on the ever-changing tide of social acceptance. But, in the off-chance of our both going at once, we wanted some protection that a bereavement-crazed relative couldn't take an end run and claim first custodial rights over our appointed guardian.

People do crazy things around death.

As illustrated in the movie. The biological mother's parents had been so open, so welcoming; they embraced their daughter's partner, until their daughter died. Then, she became "that damn dyke" and a bad influence on their granddaughter.

Ouch.

People do crazy things around illness, too, which is when those powers-of-attorney come in handy. The last time we shivered with fright after seeing a movie, it was *If These Walls Could Talk 2,* and if the second section with Chloe Sevigny playing butch turned up the heat, the first section with Vanessa Redgrave chilled us to the bone. Being turned away from the hospital because you are not "family" (as the Redgrave character is when her life partner becomes critically ill) is not something that died with the sixties. Without legal marriage, wills and powers-of-attorney are the only thing we have to place our partners first in line for decision-making and visitation should we become unable to speak for ourselves. Domestic-partner registration options are all very nice symbolically, but as our lawyer pointed out, they don't do diddly under the law.

While we have no reason to expect an irrational in-law end-run, and hope to live long and healthy lives, it would be wrong to leave any loophole unclosed, so we spent a couple of hours, and a bundle on the credit card, to protect the lives we've worked so hard to build.

Marriage would protect them even more.

No Bevy of Bridezillas Here

It poured the whole six blocks from the Smart Park on Eighth and Yamhill downtown (where we left the vans) to the First Unitarian Church on Twelfth and Main. Graeme had finally fallen asleep in the van on the way, so I carried all twenty-two pounds of him against my chest, covered in a blanket, praying he'd stay asleep and get enough rest so he wouldn't scream through any or all of the upcoming ceremonies.

We were soaked, and starving. Despite the goodies on offer during the morning, we all ate very little, too keyed up already to want a sugar buzz lending an edge to our emotions. And since we are a bunch of middle-aged ladies (two without gall bladders), we were scared to eat or drink much without a bathroom close by.

After knocking, ringing, and then pounding on the door, they let us in at the church. A few of the staff already knew about the county decision, and were ready to jump into action and whip up a wedding at a moment's notice. Chris and Lisa were nowhere to be seen (they'd stopped for flowers), and we were told that Tom was somewhere in the building getting vows together, busily retrofitting commitment ceremony lines into marriage promises. Terri assessed our needs and took off down the block to the store for sandwiches, and I held Graeme tight against me to keep him asleep, tactically evading the friendly woman who kept trying to pat him, unaware that doing so might spell disaster should he awake.

We were not exactly wedding-ready. We were dressed for the weather: thick socks, heavy shoes, coats, sweaters. Our daughter was wearing black sweatpants, and the baby was wearing the same warm, but grungy, outfit he wore to bed at eleven last night. There was no more time to fuss about clothing than the thirty seconds I gave it that morning. No six months to fret about every detail, time and opportunity turning us into a bevy of bridezillas.

This was probably a good thing.

In my twenties (and underemployed), I used to make little black dresses I could otherwise not afford, snazzy trousers, and the occasional shoulder bag. These days, I only sew couch covers, curtains, and costumes. One of my earliest jobs was at the fabric store my mother owned, which is why I'm a lesbian who sews.

Terri sews, too; she claims that sewing machines are power tools.

From time to time, when I've gone to Fabric Depot for my annual Halloween costume making marathon (dinosaurs, guinea pigs, and vampires OH MY), I've ambled the aisles before heaving bolts about, somehow finding myself in the bridal section.

Generally, the bridal section of any fabric store is a taste-free wasteland. You have to go to a *really* spendy shop for a wide selection of wearable options. But once, amongst all the hideous faux brocade, pearl beading, and too shiny polyester satin on offer at the discount store I go to for fake fur and fleece, I saw it: a lovely bolt of off-white sheer organza with my name all over it, just waiting to be made into a voluminous skirt someone could get lost in for days. Sigh.

I've had a lot of time to think about this. Given the opportunity, I could probably rethink "the dress" nine million times, sew something I end up discarding, buy something off the rack I then return, and change my mind at the last minute, going back to option one, agonizing all the way. Our spontaneous ceremony was astoundingly agony-free: no guest list to fuss over, no colors to debate, no matching bridesmaid disasters, no caterers to hire, no room to book, and no second mortgage to pay for the lot.

As Lisa said later, "We had all of the best parts of a wedding, with none of the worst."

"We're the Mothers of the Brides"

Marty's mom swept through the double doors of the sanctuary, and scuttled up the aisle, one mother of the bride ready for this day. She left Marty's dad at home; his wandering sense of place had become a challenge. Terri's family was far away; her nine brothers and sisters scattered across the country, her parents in Wisconsin, no one near enough to come. Her mother, Norma, is always with us in spirit, though; as a nurse and mother of ten, she has a rule for everything (you'd have to), and sometimes we borrow them. We say, "It's a Norma rule," and the kids know it's law.

Jannine's friend, Liz, came in: her eyes wild, her short graying hair standing on end, curly after her recent bout with cancer. She had the stunned look of a two year-old on Christmas morning—How did this happen?! She got down to the business of giving Jannine a hard time, "What do you mean calling me like this, with no advance notice? How can you just get married without planning ahead? It's not how it's done! Are you crazy?"

She was, I think, quite tickled to be Jannine's witness.

My mother made it in time, peeking around the door, unsure she was in the right church at the right time. She waved at us, came up silently to sit in the next pew, and handed me a folded antique lace handkerchief she'd remembered to bring, mouthing, "Something old," while the Minister, Tom, explained to Jannine and me what he'd come up with for vows. I tucked the handkerchief into my jeans pocket, figuring that's two: something old, something blue ...

Terri came back with the mother-load: half a dozen sandwiches, chips, cookies, a rainbow balloon, flowers, and a story.

At the grocery store, she'd cleaned out the ready-made sandwich bin, gathered some edibles, and taken them to the check stand. The clerk said it looked like she was going to a party, and Terri said no, a wedding. "Actually," Terri told her, "Three weddings." The clerk looked doubtfully at the sandwiches, the chips, and the four bouquets, "Are you the caterer?"

"No," Terri replied, "One of the brides."

Jannine took the bouquet of red roses she'd asked Terri to pick up, and presented it to me with a grin before it was whisked away by the church women taking action all around us, thinking of ways to make our ceremonies special even on a moment's notice, while grinning up to their eyes. One of them quipped, "We're the mothers of the brides!" They absconded with all the flowers, including the bouquet presented to Terri earlier with the champagne, and turned them into beautiful bridal bouquets wrapped with ribbon, a thing I'd lost hope of holding in this lifetime.

The church pianist, Signe, arrived with a bucket of long-stem red roses she bought on the way so they could be part of the wedding ceremony, symbols of our romantic love. She asked us all to pick music. Marty and Terri chose first, and by the time it was our turn to leaf through the options, it was becoming almost too complicated; Jannine and I had no idea. Under normal conditions, we'd have spent months deciding, as I made one snap decision after another, and Jannine debated the options 'till she was blue in the face, our decision-making styles highly incompatible. We let Signe surprise us.

Chris and Lisa arrived with Katie, Jacob, and more flowers. They were dressed nicely, and didn't look like they'd spent the night waiting to marry in the morning. Lisa looked sophisticated and pulled together in black pants and sweater (which she later told me was merely "work drag"; she was ready to sprint off to work if Multnomah County stopped the marriages at the last moment, and relieve the co-worker who'd stepped in to deliver babies so Lisa could marry). Chris looked like an Eddie Bauer ad in corduroy trousers and sweater, ever the absent-minded professor.

Marty and Terri had worn attractive vests under their mid-western winter wear, so they were festive and bright once they'd peeled off the top layer of Gore-Tex and goose down. Jannine and I were in jeans: she in a grey sweater, me in a black cotton top (one of dozens in my closet), which was fitting because we've never done well with fancy. We are jeans people and will likely die jeans people, and it was appropriate we should marry this way.

It was as I ate my long-awaited sandwich and guzzled a Diet Coke in the hallway that I looked at our friends: Chris and Lisa, Marty and Terri, and Jeanna and Ellen, who had arrived to witness our weddings before prepping for their own that evening, and realized that Jannine and I would have a new anniversary date, one that we shared with our best friends.

We'd had a new anniversary date before, but it didn't stick. Eight years ago, Jannine and I had the good fortune to celebrate the big 1–0 together. I say "fortune," because after all this time together, we know it's nothing we're doing consciously. We understand that all couples are just one wrong sneeze, wrong word, or wrong mood swing away from divorce, and that we are no exception.

Yet, with that depressing thought tucked away with both our individual and collective baggage, we still intended to go out and celebrate our decade together. However, any large scale plans were sort of circumvented by the fact that we weren't even sure what date to celebrate shortly before the event.

You'd think after ten years we'd know ...

We'd had a date in the past, and it was a perfectly good one: Boxing Day. It's just that we'd had one of those heavy, deep, and real conversations months before when we were discussing my endless desire for a wedding, the lack of celebration in our lives, and the meaning of anniversaries, and we'd decided to up and change our anniversary from the day after Christmas (which would be the "first kiss" anniversary) to September fifth, when we exchanged our first set of rings.

It seemed like a good idea at the time. September is a better time to get friends together, we'd been more committed to each other by then (she'd decided she could come out of the closet, and I'd decided to stop sabotaging the relationship so I could get life back to normal and date people who were bad for me), and so, during that fateful conversation that lasted until three, we changed our anniversary date.

Thus, it was a bit late in the day for elaborate plans when I approached Jannine in mid-December, tears trickling a mute plea across my face, and announced, "I want to keep our anniversary!" To Jannine's credit, even before I could pour out my litany of reasons why December twenty-sixth was a more romantic occasion, she agreed to switch back.

So, we decided to go out to dinner together, alone. As the parents of small children, being able to complete a sentence and our meal without a child in someone's lap or a five yard dash for a sponge was a thrilling event.

The evening was not without challenges, starting with where to go. One of my pet peeves is "stupid food" or what some call nouvelle cuisine: tiny portions of conflicting flavors artistically arranged for ten dollars an ounce. However, after receiving recommendations and sworn statements from three witnesses that the restaurant we'd selected served adequate or large portions, was known to include lettuce in a salad (as opposed to arugula, sorrel, rocket, or endive), and would not require that I sit cross-legged on the floor without shoes, we were good to go.

Of course, on the night itself, we had to drive smack dab into the middle of an ice storm.

OK, not smack dab in the middle, but *practically*. The roads were clear and unfrozen, but everything else was coated in ice. One could say that it added romance to the occasion: the sparkling leaves, the gleaming blades of grass, the endless downed trees, but it wouldn't be true. That we had to drive under a power line supported by two road signs ripped out of the ground and propped against cars is something that still makes me shudder. What were we doing leaving the house in that weather?

We did make it to the restaurant, and it was lovely (and far from empty, so there were other romantic fools on the road as well); it had a nice interior, warm air that blasted my frozen extremities, and a waiter who practically threw himself at our feet, so eager was he to please.

I was nervous, though. We didn't get out much, then. It was like going out on a date again. And like those early dates, I made vital strategic errors, the worst of which was discovering the hard way that anniversary night is not the time to remind one's spouse of a mutual pledge toward posture improvement. But in the end, Jannine had the grace to forgive me, and we had a good time.

In the candlelight, we held up our glasses of non-alcoholic beer, and toasted to another decade of the same: to mutual respect, to the memory of our first love for each other, and to the gleam in our children's eyes when they see us hold one another—and to not having any wrong sneezes.

The Wedding March

It was time. The Associated Press photographer who had hopefully hovered was asked, by joint bridal decision, to leave during the ceremonies. None of us were getting married in order to appear in papers across the country.

The eight kids were asked to settle down by the Senior Minister, Marilyn Sewell; not surprising since they'd been vaulting up the stairs, across the altar, and orating at the podium as if they owned the place. Which, having spent quite a bit of time there attending Sunday School, singing in the choir, ringing bells, and dressing like a sheep on Pageant day, some of them probably felt they did. We were in the old Salmon Street sanctuary, kind of English, ancient pipe organ, wooden pews, nothing too clean, just the place for women to marry on a Wednesday morning.

With some urging, the kids were finally seated, the friends and parents were pulling out tissues, Marilyn Sewell joined Tom Disrud to co-officiate, and all at once, it was happening.

On cue, Graeme was suddenly awake and hungry and potentially loud. I dove for the pile of Ritz crackers I'd brought, doling them out one by one during the ceremonies, anything to keep his mouth and hands busy.

Chris and Lisa were first, Katie and Jacob behind them. They walked up the aisle together, and already everyone, including Tom, was crying. Jacob held the rings on a pillow. Katie held flowers. Chris, always a weeper, could barely speak through her tears. During the vows, the nineteen years of love and commitment that led up to this moment was a tangible thing, a presence that everyone in the sanctuary could feel.

They exchanged rings, kissed, and were pronounced "married." We all stood as they walked back down the aisle, beaming, and were photographed in the narthex while our family moved to the rear of the church, snatching another handful of crackers on the way, to await our turn. As Marty and Terri stood up with McKenzie to begin their walk down the aisle, Chris and Lisa piled into the pew ahead of us, and Lisa grabbed Jannine's hand and squeezed, unable to express emotion any other way at that moment.

Marty and Terri walked down the aisle looking like a couple who had weathered the years, and become a comfortable, stable, loving family. Tom stumbled over some of the vows, forgetting entirely the blessing and exchanging of the rings, he was so emotional. This was a big day for him. In the rear pew, we could barely hear the vows, but we know they were slightly different from Chris and Lisa's, by accident and intention. This was no Las Vegas wedding chapel or the Church of Elvis, this was a church of community, and this was a real, if spontaneous, wedding.

Marty and Terri kissed and came back down the aisle with McKenzie, everyone standing as they passed. Marty's mother was snapping pictures, and mopping her eyes.

It was time, and Graeme was restless and still munching. He'd hardly eaten all morning, was still mad at his nursing-free state, but he'd been a trooper. My left breast was the size of a small cantaloupe as Jannine and I stood at the ready, waiting for our music to begin. I carry him on my left, so he hid this imbalance, though I am the only one who could possibly care at such a moment, among such good friends.

Duncan and Anna were remarkably calm. They both seemed to know just how serious this was and took their places with a calm dignity. The piano music began and we walked up the aisle, my black sweater covered with crumbs. The two ministers faced us. How many weddings have they performed where one of the brides is sprinkled with crackers and carries a toddler? Liz tried to dive in and grab Graeme, but we waved her away. This was the way we wanted it. The children are part of our marriage. They exist because between us we had enough love and energy to bring three children into our home and the world; there was nowhere else they should have been at that moment, but with us.

Tom messed up the vows a little, which was fitting since I was a little messy, too, and isn't the world? He asked Jannine twice to say "I will," mixing up our names at the crucial point. Not sure what to do when it was my turn to speak and Jannine had been asked again, there was a pregnant pause before I said, "I do, too, I will, I have," and the moment was saved.

Before we got to this moment, I always thought it would feel awkward saying the vows, fake somehow, like a theatre performance. Or, that I would blubber endlessly, because I am a crier like Chris, weeping over everything. Minutes before, I thought maybe it would feel clinical, since we planned to have another, more elaborate wedding later, that day allegedly being about making it legal.

But, it wasn't about that anymore. I looked into Jannine's eyes and meant every word. It was all true, and more. No tears, no awkwardness, just joy to say it there and then, with witnesses, and a license, and the blessings of our community.

We exchanged rings, platinum bands we bought two years ago, then kissed and were married, and walked back down the aisle, somehow holding hands with our kids. We realized halfway and grabbed each other's hands instead, laughing at ourselves that even in this most romantic and symbolic moment, we were thinking of the kids first.

The Day My Father Died

The day my father died, I hung up the phone after getting the news from the hospital, turned to Jannine, and told her, "We can have children now."

It would be nice if that was a testament to intergenerational relationships, but it wasn't. A cloud had lifted; a cloud I didn't even know existed, that had barred the possibility of childrearing for as long as my dad was alive.

My father was always an odd bird. I learned after his death, from his brother, that he was a rocket scientist with the military, and considered brilliant. I learned from my mother that he never seemed to get pleasure out of the things that made other people happy: friendship, affection, family, a job well done. I knew growing up that my sister was the favorite, but that wasn't a good thing to be. It meant he tried to mold her in his image, relating to her intense intelligence and awkward social tendencies. I was the dumb one in my family, less than straight A's, so not really up to standard. I may not have been his favorite, but I was his audience. He talked to me, filling my head with drug information, ribald stories, a paranoid perspective, and too many examples of his twisted sense of humor. And that was when he was sober.

When his mother died in her early nineties, my father drank continually until acute liver and kidney failure stopped him the day before he turned sixty. His father, for whom Richards Avenue in Norwalk, Connecticut, is named (home of the Danbury Mint, maker of hand painted plates of dubious design), outlived him by a year.

I hadn't seen him for a year or two before I got the call that he was at Harborview Hospital, and dying. Tired of conversations that turned to sex, drugs, and mental illness within five minutes (and you could time it), I had broken away, going so far as to change my name and move in order to make the break. Even at his deathbed (after he'd recovered enough from the delirium tremens to converse), he enjoyed playing cat and mouse, urging Jannine to go on a search for money he'd stuck up a pipe. When we asked how he'd gotten it up such a narrow place, he replied that he was "the snake man, the snake man," enjoying the effect of his words.

By the time he was dying, he'd been a lonely man, rejected by the children he'd terrorized, abandoned by his tavern buddies (none of whom came to see him while he lay near death for ten days), and a stranger to his family, who conveniently waited until he was good and dead to be in contact. On one of our last phone calls before they found him on his apartment floor, naked, and waiting to die, in a litter of bottles, and urine, and blood, he asked me if I had a boyfriend, and I said no. Then, he asked if I had a girlfriend. I said, yes, wondering what his response would be. When I was in high school, he told me he thought homosexuality was caused by an over density of population, like with rats. But, on the phone, he just paused for a moment, and said, "Good, it's a terrible thing to be alone."

I'm skeptical of heaven and hell, but seeing my father as he lay dying, trying to pull the tubes from his body in his eagerness to get it over with and die, I could believe in an afterlife. He looked like a man who sees the hounds of hell pursuing him. I suspect that his Methodist upbringing was coming back to him those last days, and as he looked at my sister and me, some glimpse of a different path came to him. His teeth were rotting in his mouth, so he was hard to understand, but at one point he looked at me and said, "I missed so much."

When the phone call came that he had actually died, that the man I thought would be haunting me into my sixties, arriving unexpectedly and drunk at a special occasion, or calling in the middle of the night for money, it changed my world. No longer would I fear for myself, or children I might have. There was no "grandpa" who might show up asking for access, no poisonous influence touching a new generation. The break I had never been able to manage on my own (feeling even on his death bed as if I should be feeding my youth, life, and energy to him, as if he literally owned me), was done. We could have children.

Jannine, on the other hand, had always wanted to have children. She came into our relationship with a Ward and June agenda: monogamy, employment, home-owning, parenthood, in that order. Three and a half years later, we'd accomplished three of the items on her list. We were still together and lived in our own little condominium with a view (if you stood on a chair and squinted). There was only one thing we were missing.

When my father died, I knew she was right. We could have a child. And should. Eight months later, to the day, we were pregnant. We might have gotten going even sooner, but there were things to take care of, like reconciling Jannine to the fact that she was going to get what she'd always wanted.

When the plan was a go, I promptly left my delightful, but unreliable art gallery job and landed a sit-down customer service position with benefits at Airborne Express. I was good at it, setting speed records for how fast I could finish a call with a happy customer. The day the benefits kicked in, was the day we got pregnant.

I was able to keep my condition hidden until my six month evaluation, when I finally told my supervisors. They were pretty surprised. First one said, "I didn't know you were married," and I said I wasn't; then the other one asked, "How does your boyfriend feel about it?" and I said I didn't have one.

But, I didn't 'fess up. Our insemination coincided approximately with a trip to see Jannine's buddy, Andy, off to the first Gulf War in Kuwait. I left my employers with the vague impression that I got into the spirit of seeing the boys off to war, and had no idea who the father was. The fleet was in.

Thirteen years later, I still blush with shame for this lie of omission, but I worked my booty off while I was there, which was up until two weeks before Duncan was born. There were no partner benefits back then; we wanted to have a baby, and not go broke in the process.

But, we ended up with three.

After we'd managed to bring two children into the world, barely juggling all the cacophony that created, Duncan still kept on us to "go to the hospital and get another baby." It wasn't that he was hot to trade in his sister. He loved her. He would throw himself in front of her car seat and tell people, "I'm very protective." He just wanted another. There we were, ready to retire from the procreating ring and he kept wanting to bring us back for a rematch. Luckily, since we're lesbians, we don't do accidents, or I'd be a mother of ten. But the seed was planted, and I never gave up wanting to see it grow.

By the time we decided to have Graeme (Jannine finally agreeing in a post-hysterectomy surge of life lust that I was right, we should have more children), no one would ever believe the fleet was in.

Graeme Had Had Enough

While we had our picture taken after the ceremony, our friends Cindy and Teri arrived, and were talking to Tom about getting married. They'd already had a big church wedding some years earlier, but they wanted to make it legal ASAP.

Graeme and I didn't wait around to see their exchange of vows. He'd had it. Jannine and the older kids stayed, but Graeme and I skedaddled into the hallway so Cindy and Teri wouldn't have their marriage overshadowed by lusty cries and struggles. It was a relief to put him down, for both of us. He toddled around happily, exploring the linoleum floor, finding treasures he thought might be edible, and I thought might obstruct his airways.

The ceremony seemed to take forever since I was trying to hush a long-suppressed toddler, who wasn't taking a hint. We moved far down the hallway to lessen his echoing squeals. Before long, the wooden double doors swung open, and the kids poured out into the hallway and swooped on the remnants of lunch like well-behaved hyenas. My mother came out, along with Marty's mom, clutching well-used handkerchiefs. Liz was still keyed up, waiting around to sign our certificate as an official witness, before dashing back to the office, blocks away.

The brides all moved to the Channing Room, a formal parlor with wing chairs and a fireplace, where the ministers signed the marriage licenses, and we swapped signatures on each other's forms, bearing witness to one another's weddings. The cameraman was there, filming the signing, eager to capture something after being banned from the ceremonies.

Graeme was now on the loose, moving from chair to chair, examining each for climbing potential, and attempting an ascent. Our accoutrements had somehow grown during the long morning; we now had bouquets to carry, paperwork, cameras, and coats. The signing seemed to take a long time, but it's what makes a wedding legal, so it was worth every ever-vigilant second of keeping Graeme from breaking a church heirloom, or his own neck. Finally, we'd shaken hands with the ministers, the friends had dispersed, and the mothers had headed home to call everyone in the extended family they could think of. There was a collective sense of "what next?"

How We Came
to Know These Women

We met all these newlyweds through a lesbian moms group.

When we considered moving to Portland *very* suddenly eleven and a half years ago (as in, "Hey honey, this job opened up, how would you like to move to Portland?"), little did I realize I would have three weeks to get us packed up, an apartment rented, our house in Tacoma ready to rent, and my spouse psychologically prepared to start a new job. I didn't have time to realize that we'd be landing in a city where we had no social contacts except a couple of exes once removed (nice gals with whom we had little in common), and ex-boyfriend number two, heck of a nice guy and always up for a cup of coffee, but not a lesbian mom, and, to the best of my knowledge, never likely to be one.

We were two moms with a toddler son, three cats, and two canaries; we needed peers in a big way.

Making friends once you have kids is a whole new ball game. If you want to meet someone pre-parenting, you have endless options. You may not like them all, but they exist. You can hang out at cafés, you can idle in the grocery store, and you can stop and chat with interesting people when you meet them. While you enjoy an exchange of ideas you can categorize them in your mind: a) friend-to-be, b) absolutely incompatible, c) somewhere in between.

With young kids, you're lucky to get to pay for that latte, much less linger, chat, or think clearly enough to categorize further than animal, vegetable, or mineral, and you'll probably have food (or worse) smeared across your left shoulder while you're doing that.

Knowing that we were in some serious need of contemporaries, we checked out the local gay/lesbian/bisexual/transgender newspaper, *Just Out*.

In it, we found a "Lesbians with Kids" group advertised, though when we went, it felt more like "Moms pretending to not have children, want to participate in our denial?" We only went to one or two meetings. Being new mothers, we were appalled that the goal of this group (who had school-age children) was to get away from their kids more often, not wallow in mother love.

Not that they were bad mothers, they loved their kids, read the right parenting books, and bought organic milk. They were just different than we were in their outside-of-children interests—they had them. They said they felt like they needed to be away from their children in order to be gay, something we could never fathom. They talked about two-step dances and hiking excursions, and warned us of the dangers of spending too much energy on junior, and not enough on ourselves.

Of course we scoffed, wanting no part of this attitude that children chewed you up like a candy bar, and your life could be swallowed up whole. We were blissfully naïve.

We checked *Just Out* again, and found "The Lesbian Mothers Group," with instructions on where to meet and when. From the first, this was a better fit. The kids were closer in age to our son, the mothers were as hyper-involved as we were, and we made several lasting friendships over the years we brunched together on a monthly basis.

Meanwhile, society trudged on, and in those five years, amazing things happened (like our daughter Anna arriving): adoptions for lesbians and gays became more common, fertility clinics started catering to us, the gayby boom was in full swing, and it became not a statistical impossibility to find more than one child of lesbians or gay men in a classroom. Other parents we met *got it* about us right away, and didn't blink an eye. We found ourselves hanging with the preschool moms, or having social gatherings with the soccer parents. The kids got older, and concerns we had about being the only family like this blew away in a collective sigh of relief.

Interest in the group dwindled, folks volunteered to help less, and brunch-goers tended to have conflicts with church attendance, which finally led Lisa, who'd been keeping the group going, to do a phone survey to assess the level of interest. She let everyone know she was ready for someone else to take it on, and when no one volunteered, ultimately decided to drop the ball and see if anyone cared enough to pick it up.

No one did.

Jannine and I had a hard time letting it go, but we weren't about to pick up that ball and run with it. So, we began our own tradition of hosting a potluck shortly after Thanksgiving, to keep some of us meeting on a regular basis, if only annually.

I don't remember that first gathering well, it has disappeared in a sleep deprived fog (Anna was still a lap baby at the time). I only know that we made a turkey and cranberry sauce with orange rind, our friends showed up, there was much laughter, the children spent five minutes eating and four hours playing, and we got to spend time with our friends when we could really talk for a change.

One year, by the time it was over, the kids had been playing for six hours and the youngest ones were begging to be allowed to go to bed! Another year, we broke out in an impromptu chorus of "The Age of Aquarius." Two years ago, I had at least three medically-minded moms urging me to let someone else lift the twenty-four pound turkey in and out of the oven since I was big with child.

For the kids, this annual feast is special. There are the older children, leading the pack in knowledge about Harry Potter, PG-13 movies, the existence of Santa Claus, and the mysteries of sex. There are the middle ones, satisfied to play, sandwiched between these demi-gods, and the toddling upstarts that sit on their mothers' knees and remind the other moms of those bygone days of babies, diapers, and symbiotic love. These kids go to different schools, are in different grades, the only thing they have in common are lesbian moms, which for the most part has been no big deal. But later, I hope these kids create a network of support for each other, if tough times come, and questioning begins. When they get angry at being different, or hurt by the words of others.

These women have taught me a lot about parenthood. We share the struggles with school administrators, with doctors who look at us blankly and say, "He can't have two mothers," with trying to keep our relationships going during the marathon race of high maintenance child rearing. We are resources for each other on swim teachers, art camps, dog breeds, and the side effects of obscure antibiotics. We are, in effect, that extended family of old, part of the village it takes to raise a child, made from a new model.

Plus, once in a while, reminding each other, with a twinkle and a knowing smile, of the lives we led before we were happily immersed in minivan heaven.

What Now?

The ink wasn't dry on our marriage license when flowers arrived at our house. While we were making our weary way home from the church (it wasn't even one o'clock in the afternoon), our neighbor, Carol, was leaving a message on our voice mail asking if we'd had "a happy event?"

At Marty and Terri's house across the street, flowers were waiting on the steps. At Chris and Lisa's house, a neighbor had delivered wine and an enormous flowering shrub. We arrived at our house after a pit stop at the County Building to rescue the chairs, dragged our exhausted and elated selves into the house, and collapsed.

The vans were a mess of chairs, air mattresses, sleeping bags, and uneaten granola bars, but that could wait. Duncan and Anna went off to play Game Cube with McKenzie, while Marty and Terri recovered for a moment in the privacy of their home. Soon, they were over at our house, and Lisa, too, coming through the door carrying bags of eclectic groceries she'd gathered from home. In a post-traumatic mania, she began whipping up eggs, pancakes, and hash browns for everyone at our house, while Chris slept on the couch at home and their kids joined the Game Cube crowd upstairs.

Jannine and I could only sit there at our old round kitchen table, alternately catatonic with wonder and wildly verbal as we rehashed this synergistic experience we had just been through; the sum total of the waiting, the emotion, and the sharing of these precious moments far greater than its parts.

Graeme was in his high chair, wolfing down milk, yogurt, and scrambled eggs. He'd been too stimulated to eat while in line, too tired in the car, too disoriented at the church (except for that handful of Ritz crackers which will always remain in my memory, and possibly in that of the church janitor's as well). Now, he was scarfing too much, too fast. He coughed, sneezed, or just burped, and everything he'd eaten came out in a stream of milky baby vomit that cascaded through my long hair, over my shoulder, and onto Lisa's coat.

So experienced were the parents sitting around the table that not one person blanched or even paused. They smiled and went on eating, while Jannine dropped her jaw and grabbed a towel to begin clearing up the wreckage. Into the wash went Lisa's coat. Into the shower I went. Graeme got a washing up for which he was long overdue, considering the ground he'd been crawling over.

While I was in the shower, three bouquets arrived, two from parents at Anna's school, and one from our friend and neighbor, Megan, who came in and joined us at the kitchen table to enjoy our collective buzz, hear the story firsthand, and glory in our county's liberal progress. With a fresh coat of paint, and smelling a whole lot better, I rejoined the crew in time to help finish the recap for Megan, accept her hearty congratulations, and resume my lunch.

After Megan left, the question around the table was: what do we do from here? Is this it?

Lisa leaned back in her chair, and said, "I don't know about you gals, but I feel good and married."

Jannine nodded. "Me, too," I said, "I thought we'd want to do it again, but no, that was just right." Terri and Marty were nodding, too.

We had, all of us, thought that maybe we'd have another ceremony later, a few days later, or a couple of weeks, to allow relatives and friends from far away who would like to come, to come. Jannine and I had spoken to Tom Disrud about saving time the following Saturday, thinking we'd schedule it soon to better ensure it happening before the county stopped issuing licenses, which wouldn't necessarily invalidate our marriage, but would have made any ceremony anti-climactic as heck.

We all felt that it would be redundant to do it again. Yet, as the phone calls came, we felt some sort of celebration was in order. Sleep deprivation making us indecisive, we shelved that topic, and Lisa suggested we needed cake.

Wedding cake for Jeanna and Ellen's wedding that evening.

I got on the phone and called bakeries optimistically, and they laughed when I asked how soon a wedding cake could be thrown together. After the fifth try, an actual wedding cake was out, but we knew Costco was always good for tasty sheet cakes, and Lisa offered to go.

In fact, Lisa seemed to need to go, go, go. We all deal with the unexpected in different ways. All Jannine wanted was to crash, Marty and Terri had snuck off to sleep on our couch, and I wanted to make darn sure Graeme had a good nap before we tried to take him to any more weddings. Anna had money to spend on canned food for the food bank collection at school, so since Costco is the place for canned tuna and beans, she went with Lisa and Katie, where they bought sheet cakes, seltzer water, and an impulse purchase television/DVD/VCR combo which imploded months later when a bolt of lightning struck their house.

Jacob, McKenzie, and Duncan played video games upstairs, unaware of any of this, while the rest of us went into sleep mode.

By the time we got to the First Unitarian church that night, we were showered, dressed up, and reasonably rested.

I didn't get to see Jeanna and Ellen's exchange of vows, though. The second the doors of the Channing Room closed for their ceremony, Graeme began struggling and let out a piercing shriek that bounced off the walls and echoed through the building. He'd had quite enough of weddings for one day, and wasn't going to be silenced. Since Jeanna and Ellen were one of three couples getting married back to back, I escaped quickly with him to the church toddler room for the duration.

As I hustled Graeme down the hall, I passed two local reporters and a camera man grumbling about not being allowed in for the ceremony, saying what was wrong with these people anyway, not letting them in when they'd been sent down to the church to cover the story? As if our weddings were only news.

After the ceremonies, Lisa brought out the cakes from Costco, and set them on tables in the same hallway we'd had lunch in that day. All the kids were in remarkably good humor considering what they'd all been through, and their own lack of sleep. Jannine and I were already pondering the possibility of wedding presents for our three. Seven weddings in a day is a lot for any kid (or adult), and after we ate a great deal of cake, we were all ready to call it a night.

The New York Times
Publishes Same-Sex Weddings

When I crawled out of bed the next morning and grabbed the newspaper off the front porch before my loved ones awoke, I saw that there was no need for us to tell anyone in town that we'd gotten married. The whole front page of the paper was wedding announcement enough, even without our names. There were editorials, letters to the editor, feature stories, personal interest pieces, and photographs. I turned to my daily dose of comics, and avoided the issue while I could.

But it occurred to me, were we going to send in a wedding announcement? What would it say? Did we have to?

Then I wondered, if we did send one in, would the *Oregonian* even print it under Weddings, or under their recently added Commitments section, since we were a same-sex couple? Would they change their existing policy, wait until the dust clears, or until the issue goes to the State Supreme Court? They'd have to declare a policy because announcements were going to pour in.

The *New York Times* made their decision in the summer of 2002 to include same-sex wedding announcements, legal or no.

At the time it was a tiny, three-paragraph blurb in the *Oregonian* that caught my attention as I reeled over my morning beverage from yet another story about a kidnapped child turning up dead. It had been a hell of a summer that way. The headline read "*New York Times* will print news of same-sex unions," announcing the about-face of the *New York Times*, who would recognize us gay folks in the Sunday Styles section, after earlier refusing to do so, along with other notables being wed.

I thought, as I slurped my decaf, "It's about time."

Jannine, upon hearing the news, said that the mystery was why they weren't doing it long ago, printing announcements of our unions. She had a point.

It was New York after all: home of Stonewall, home of the biggest gay pride parade going, home of Rudy Giuliani staying with gay pals when his former marriage unraveled, home of fashion week, and true seasons, and rules involving the wearing of white. Unions must be celebrated every day, and not just between Joe

Blow and Bill Doe, but between city official X and socialite J, with all the trimmings, weddings that should make the paper (if any wedding is really news), whether the couple is gay, straight or in-between.

That morning I took it as a beacon of hope, a sign that the world was finally adapting to our existence, and that we wouldn't forever have to sit back and accept our second-class citizenship with a smile.

Naturally, the *New York Times* left itself room to maneuver, the article stated that the couples featured would be selected "under the same criteria used to choose the weddings: the newsworthiness and accomplishments of the couples and their families."

This had me worried at the time, considering the moral and ethical effect this might have on same-sex couples in New York City: would they suddenly become obsessed with making it into *The Times* like their straight counterparts? Would big, glamorous weddings involving wedding planners, live swans, and Annie Liebovitz behind the lens become *de rigueur*? Would the gay scions of wealthy families who vacation at Martha's Vineyard (or wherever *the* vacation spot is these days, I'm a west coaster and middle class, so what do I know?) suddenly become pressured to find a nice boy and settle down, so Mummy could have her moment of glory? Would the formerly embarrassing dyke daughters of politicians be introduced to pretty debutantes in the hopes of a mutually beneficial alliance? Would blue-blooded gay and lesbian singles suddenly be pawns in the game of Society Life, like their straight siblings before them?

But my sympathy for the wealthy scion sons and Society daughters pressured into same-sex alliances didn't last long. From this coast, it seemed a small price for them to pay so the rest of us could pick up the paper, and think, "Now, this is progress!"

A Reception in Two Days?

When I walked Anna into Alameda School later that morning, Graeme on my hip, mothers stopped us to say they'd seen us on the news, and congratulations. Anna enjoyed handing her note to her teacher—"Please excuse Anna's absence on Wednesday, March 3rd, she had to attend her parents' wedding"—she smiled up at Mr. McElroy as he read it. His eyebrows went up, he grinned, and said, "Wow, congratulations!" shaking hands all around.

As Graeme and I walked up to Duncan's school, Fernwood, his teacher, Mrs. Wong (literature/language arts/social studies block), was getting out of her car. She raced up to us, "I saw you on the news! Congratulations!" then grabbed Duncan and hugged him enthusiastically, then hugged me.

He brought his note into the school office, the secretary automatically murmuring, "You were sick?" without even bothering to read the note he held out in his hand. Duncan shook his head, indicating the note. She read it. "Oh!" she said, "Well, well, congratulations."

I was grateful to get Graeme back home after delivering his siblings, and thought seriously about collapsing on the bed. The house was a wreck, dishes were piled high, detritus from the van was covering the dining table, and a ramshackle wedge of flowers left over from the marriage marathon was stuck in a bucket of water on the kitchen counter. I decided to tackle the flowers first, putting Graeme into the backpack to keep him out of trouble.

Jannine had been a little nervous going back to work. She knew that all her work-mates knew about our marriage from the e-mails that filled her in-box the previous day, not just the ones she had e-mailed about her potential absence, and that not everyone would be happy about it. Yet, an enthusiastic crowd gathered around her desk shortly after she arrived, full of well wishes. She was astounded at the people who were happy for her, even when they were opposed to same-sex marriage. One woman stopped to congratulate her in the hallway, saying she didn't believe in it, but she was happy for Jannine because she knew it made her happy.

Jannine was not surprised that some people were ominously silent on the subject, scrupulously avoiding eye contact when the subject came up. Later, as with any marriage around the office, a card went round for signatures, and she was presented at a staff meeting with a weekend at the coast for the whole family as a wedding present.

Jannine called to check in, immediately getting to the issue on both of our minds. Should we throw a party, have a reception, do something?

All over town, same-sex newlyweds were struggling with the same questions. How do we make this meaningful and personal, how do we mark this miraculous occasion, how do we start to honor something so momentous, with only a moment's notice? Gay and lesbian organizations were trying to decide whether to throw one big party for all the newly married, or stage mass marriages like in San Francisco, or otherwise honor the day.

Lisa soon called about the same thing. Chris had talked to Jannine about throwing a party, and Lisa had gotten the job of following up. She'd already spoken to the church about possibly using their hall on Saturday. Did we want to use it together, and if we did, shouldn't all the couples who got married at the church that day, or during the days following, celebrate together?

This made a lot of sense, but didn't feel quite right. Not only because my barefoot children/big skirt fantasy was something I felt too shy to indulge in in front of the other couples who would get married that week, or that as a wishy-washy Unitarian I would feel guilty for being feted among better, more dedicated church-goers, but because it all seemed like too much to think about.

It all seemed like too much to Jannine, too, and to Lisa; when we got together with their family at the end of the day for a casual spaghetti dinner at their house, she seemed a little shell shocked. There had been a lot of publicity for them (Chris was on public radio giving an interview that day), because they were plaintiffs in the years-long lawsuit resulting in the landmark "Tanner v. OHSU" decision giving Oregon state employees benefits for same-sex partners. All this attention was both a joy and a challenge.

Chris and Lisa ended up having an open house on Saturday for their friends. Bottles of wine were brought, and much laughter ensued, though sadly, family couldn't be there. I suspect that Lisa's wedding fantasy, far from my accessorized script, involved her family filling the pews and doing those special tasks the church women had so miraculously taken on, and that is not how it went down. Not being able to have family there was definitely a downside to our hasty vows.

Marty and Terri had already started planning their celebration with Marty's mom. Since Tom forgot the blessing of their rings, they went out and bought new rings for him to bless, and had already scheduled a rooftop reception at Marty's parents' retirement home in two weeks' time that would include a blessing of the rings, a bridal dance, champagne toasts, a buffet, and more than one wedding cake.

It wasn't until the next morning, Friday, that we decided, yes, we were going to do this; we would have an open house reception, not at the church, not at a hall, but at our own house on Sunday.

We had two days.

First, there were the phone calls. I kept generating names of people we wanted to invite based on who I ran into or what name popped into my head, too scattered and sleep deprived to think logically and perhaps consult our address book to ensure we missed no one. Jannine, bless her, manned the phones between work and organizing photos for a chronological montage of our relationship. I ordered Maid Brigade for Saturday morning (this was surely the right time to throw money at a problem), and arranged for Jannine to get a badly needed haircut.

When Jannine gets a haircut, I have to go along. She can't even take the kids for haircuts because when she takes them, they come back with bowl cuts, unflattering blunt bobs, or asymmetrical trims it takes weeks to grow out and an expensive second cut to fix. When it comes to herself, she's worse. Left alone, she would wave her hands around mutely or mutter, "Um, I want it shorter." I come along to direct, sometimes with a drawing or photo of what she wants to come away with. This works.

It was on the way to the hair salon that we exchanged the only harsh words during this emotionally-charged experience. I confessed that I hadn't *exactly* told my mother that we didn't want to have the family reception she'd offered. Jannine (rightly) thought that we'd come to a joint decision. She was sure she didn't want to exert pressure on my extended family to stretch their budgets and stress their schedules, or worse, put a strain on family ties. All she wanted was a Hallmark and warm wishes.

I was waffling because I wanted to be nice to my mother, and I agreed with her that my cousins and aunts would want to come through, if they could. They are nice folks. But I agreed with Jannine that it was unreasonable to expect my cousins, especially, to drop everything and expensively haul their large families up to Vancouver, Washington, from California, to toast us with non-alcoholic champagne for an event that was over in the blink of an eye, they weren't even invited to, and may have already been declared legally nonexistent.

Jannine was exasperated I hadn't put my foot down. She appreciated the enthusiasm and good will with which the offer was made, but she was firm that down the foot must go. We went into the salon in a huff. I let the hairstylist know what Jannine wanted and took Graeme off grumpily to the other end of the salon.

She came out nicely coifed, and in a better humor. I told her I'd call, that she was right about what we should do. She acknowledged my tough spot, and how great it was that my mother came through, and made me so happy with her joy and enthusiasm. In our first years, an altercation like this could have resulted in silence for days. After a decade, it could have been a vale of tears and a three hour talk in the car. After fifteen, we started to know when to stop sweating the small stuff.

Anna Goes to Matisse

On Saturday morning I raced around picking up all over our main floor (Graeme once again strapped on my back, poor lad), hauling piles wholesale to the basement, and stuffing the cabinets in our mudroom, so that the Maid Brigade women wouldn't have to spend their valuable time cleaning around our detritus. The upstairs rooms I'd vacuumed the day before and given a brief once over, since as the kid zone during the reception, they weren't in dire need of spotlessness, though, my in-laws would be sleeping up there that night.

One of the many great things about my mother-in-law is that she doesn't think cleanliness is next to godliness. She doesn't think any less of a person if her home is bedlam. In fact, I think she rather likes it.

The older kids watched cartoons in innocence, happy in the knowledge that their beloved grandparents were arriving that afternoon, and unconscious of my frantic desire to get our house under control. I was recklessly recycling piles of paperwork (praying they didn't include bills, checks, or tax info), when, with a flash of insight, I realized we'd failed to contact an entire branch of Jannine's family who live locally, and should have been called pronto when we decided belatedly to celebrate our marriage.

I appeared in Jannine's office doorway. "Auntie Maureen! We forgot Auntie Maureen!"

Jannine gasped and grabbed the phone. Maureen answered right away, and without hesitation offered up all kinds of help. She is what Sharon Osbourne might have been had she come to America and given Ozzie a pass: a lovely Englishwoman, flashy, but tasteful, well-preserved and fit, absolutely up to date with fashion, technology, and movies, yet still a lady. We are her girls.

Maureen told Jannine quite firmly that we needed to call her sons, Sean and Russ, and invite them as well; they'd absolutely want to come. If there was anything else she could do or bring, just give her a call. She rocks.

Jannine got back on the phone, obediently, to call those cousins. I got back to clearing debris, hoping to be ready by the time our own personal cleaning crew arrived.

Maid Brigade showed up an hour and a half after I was told they would. By then, I was pacing, the baby on my back, and the kids were perched nervously on the edge of their chairs, definitely aware that I was trying to get our house under control, and ready to take off at a moment's notice, leaving the maids a clear deck to swab. The estimate for the job was breathtaking, but finding the time and energy to clean the house sufficiently to host we had no idea how many people, was beyond my capability.

Just shaving my legs was a lofty goal; we had a needy toddler in the house, he'd been separated from my breasts, he had no intention of being separated from the rest of me. Tidy I could manage with a body strapped to mine, genuinely clean was hard.

When the two women finally arrived, hauling vacuums and cleaning supplies up our steps, we sped out the door. It was half an hour to when Grandma and Grandpa would arrive on the train from Seattle.

I was secretly bummed out that I didn't have something thrilling to wear the next day. I'd stopped needing to be Rita Hayworth in a red dress, and I never needed to be princess for a day, but I did need to believe this was a big deal. Just dragging something preexisting out of the closet was anti-climactic.

Fortunately, Jannine can be something of a mind reader (one of her many lovable qualities), so she suggested that, since we had a couple of minutes to spare, why not go by Matisse, my favorite intimidating upscale clothing store, and see if they might have something I couldn't live without.

Jannine parked, and Anna hopped out with me, while the boys waited in the van.

It is ironic that I often mentally accuse my mother of low self-esteem disguised as thrift (choosing the three ninety-nine frosting kit by Clairol, instead of going for the five ninety-nine bottle of L'Oreal), when I have the same issue. It took me three separate turns through Target to buy my twenty-two dollar Cruella deVille shoes (black patent leather, pointed toe, silver buckle, kitten heel), until I finally told myself, "If I don't wear sexy shoes now, when will I wear them?" to justify the purchase.

Anna doesn't have this problem. She doesn't measure her desire for an object against her innate value as a human being, and can enter boutiques like Matisse with none of the insecurity I carry around like Jacob Marley's chains and strong boxes, sure that she has just as much right to be there as anyone else.

I was nervous about having a girl when we knew she was coming ten years ago. My family is littered with hurtful mother/daughter relationships, and I feared becoming one more Mommy Dearest branching out from the family tree. Clearly, I was no one to give her dating advice when it came to boys.

I had a strange sort of psychic experience while pregnant with her. I was lying in the bathtub, fretting about typical pregnancy problems: discomfort, emotional upheavals, getting big, and this strong female voice said, "Don't fight me, I'm coming." Swayed by hormones, I knew it was Anna speaking, that we'd be having a girl (which later ultrasounds confirmed), and that she would be smart and strong. More rationally, it was my internal voice saying, "Cool it, girl, just roll with this pregnancy thing, it's all part of the process."

I'm not entirely averse to the psychic explanation; I had an experience with Duncan as a toddler when, in desperate need of a shower, I left him in front of the television while I bathed quickly, only to have the words, "He has a knife," flash through my brain. I jumped out of the shower, ran naked down the hallway of the apartment we were living in at the time, and into the kitchen, where I found him standing on a chair holding a sharp knife he'd just taken from the kitchen drawer. Anna just started that psychic connection early.

We walked into Matisse, a mother/daughter team, with a mission.

In Matisse, everything is expensively pretty and pretty expensive, and I wear an extra large, while in real life I wear a size six. The women who work there are kind, if exceedingly skinny, and when I came in one time to exchange a birthday gift, the saleslady held Graeme while I tried sweaters on, cheerfully dragging out toys for him to play with.

The saleslady behind the antique desk looked vaguely familiar, and we soon discovered our kids went to the same school, which put us on a more level playing field—we were Alameda moms (who generally fall into the "hyper-involved/ SUV driving/middle-to-upper income/politically active/socially liberal/fighting middle age spread with a vengeance" category). She asked what I was looking for, told her I was going to a wedding reception—mine—and she was all over it. I told her that after seventeen years, it had finally happened. She said it was about time he got it together, and I corrected her with "She." Her face lit up. "Ah," she said, "Now, I know why it took so long! We've had a few women in this week getting outfits for your kind of wedding." She started pulling out skirts and shirts, and within fifteen minutes, I was out of there with a white voluminous skirt that was exactly what I was looking for.

Jannine didn't even look at the price tag, another of her lovable qualities. She just looked, smiled, nodded and told me to get in the van. It was time to get her parents.

Why Would You
Want To Do That?

These days, when we go over a river and through the woods, to Seattle, we are engulfed in a cocoon of grandparent enthusiasm. Our kids, waking from their driving-induced slumber, come alive at the idea of Grandma! Grandpa! And all the excellent electronics they stock in grandchild heaven.

Grandma will pick them up, shake them about, get down on the floor with them, and ask them (with the attention of a well-paid therapist) about everything going on in their lives. Grandpa, after initial greetings, will ask about our drive, how our new car is working out, are we hungry? He'll tell us about the projects Grandma has him working on, and ask Jannine if she'd like to go to the store with him because he forgot to get the rocky road ice cream.

Somewhere in there, Grandma will have gone off to her bedroom and come back with a shopping bag with junior-sized sweatpants, a sparkly shirt for our daughter, maybe a gross of socks, or a Lego building set. Just something she picked up, she'll say with a good-natured grin, her eyes twinkling, knowing we think our children are spoiled enough as it is.

And that's just the first twenty minutes.

How things have changed.

Whereas now they cannot wait to see our kids, initially, they weren't sure we should be having them, period.

When Jannine and I first got together, she was a good girl. She'd done nothing more boat-rocking than buying her motorcycle (she took the safety class, did the market research, and didn't buy more bike than she could handle), and had never given her parents cause for concern—no wild parties, no binge drinking, no boys named "Fang."

And then, she brought me home.

By the time I walked into their suburban-style living room replete with crystal stemware and early American furniture, I was well ensconced in the gay subculture, from cowboy boots to leather jacket, from flat top fade to attitude.

We were a cautionary tale of opposites attract. Probably still are, though my hair is down my back and I wear the boots under long skirts, to church.

Needless to say, her parents weren't overjoyed that their daughter was a lesbian (she said), and that she brought home this alarming girl for their approval, and to every holiday, birthday, family occasion, and casual Sunday drop-over ever since.

To their credit, they never considered disavowing her, throwing me out, or being openly rude. But, they weren't exactly enthused. Her father has a live and let live philosophy; he may not have been happy with the situation, but it was her life. Her mother expressed her displeasure in subtle ways: suggesting at family functions that Jannine was secretly engaged to her friend Andy, giving us two coffee makers one Christmas (just in case), and asking us not to tell anyone in the extended family.

Jannine, being young, went along with all this for a few years, hoping they would adjust. We went to endless gatherings knowing that as pleasant and polite as they were, they really didn't want us together, and would have quietly celebrated had I fulfilled their expectations and decamped.

When we decided to have a baby, we didn't have high hopes for their reaction.

We tried to be optimistic. Jannine and I came over to her parents' house one sunny weekend morning in March, 1991, intending to break the big news. We all were chatting in the kitchen amicably, when Jannine blurted out, "We're thinking about having a baby."

Her mother's face scrunched in a moue of distaste.

"Why would you want to do that?" she sneered.

Where do you go from there? Jannine tried to explain her longing for a family, her hope for the future, her gratitude for the way she was raised, but it was hard to scramble over the emotional hurdle of "why would you want to do that?" When we admitted that we were already pregnant, and that I was having the baby, they didn't offer any congratulations, only concerns.

And it hurt.

They were scared. How did they know I wasn't just using their daughter to get what I wanted? How did they know I wouldn't have the baby and then take off? Thirteen years ago, the legal prospects for non-biological parents weren't good. But, we'd done our homework. We already had an appointment to make wills, and to start Jannine's adoption of our coming son, though it was painful to be explaining safeguards in case I was a schmuck, when we should have been celebrating a grandchild.

They did their best to get used to the idea. Grandma and Grandpa put in an appearance at the baby shower, made joking references to my enlarged condition, and speculated wildly as to the identity of our anonymous donor (we had all the men at the baby shower wear "not the donor" buttons so they wouldn't be harassed).

When Duncan was born, this tenuous relationship was tested. I was a new mother, afraid for this life entrusted to us, and became The Safety Queen (a.k.a. Madame Paranoia), ever conscious of household poisons, unlocked toilets, marbles, poinsettias, food allergies, and light sockets. My in-laws' house seemed like a cesspool of danger (as did the entire world), and I let them know it, with, I regret, no tact whatsoever.

Equally, our child rearing methods appalled them. They believed in bottles, cribs, and naps timed to the microsecond. That Duncan ate nothing but breast milk until one, slept with us, was never put down, and rarely babysat, seemed weird to them, which they weren't afraid to share.

They may have been threatened by our lifestyle, but I was equally threatened by theirs. I was incredibly insecure as a new mother. Jannine's mom has dedicated her life to her children, and virtually raised her grandson, Kevin, one year older than Duncan. She could run a home with her hands tied behind her back; she's great with kids and is naturally playful, something I clearly lack.

Yet, we are very alike, she and I. We are women who want desperately to have a stable, safe, and wholesome home life, despite unstable beginnings.

It was ten years ago, as we stood side by side one summer morning at six, holding running water hoses, wearing only red plastic firefighter hats and our nightgowns, the two toddler boys playing in the wet grass, that the cracks in our mutual armor started to show, and we began to have a sense of humor about the situation.

She realized I wasn't going anywhere, and that it could be worse. I could have been a diesel dyke in steel toed boots, instead of a long-haired liberal arts major in lipstick—surely the lesser of two evils in her eyes, and easier to explain to the neighbors. I started to see the ways they'd welcomed us in, lent their support despite concerns, and loved our kids. We all started laughing at my Safety Queen status. I sided with my mother-in-law in every argument, and made meals with my father-in-law's particular tastes in mind.

They weren't quite there when we told them Anna was coming, "Oh …" but, by the time Jannine called to tell them Graeme was due in February, her mom's voice was giggling across the line, "I knew it, I knew it! I knew Beren was going to talk you into it! This is great!"

And it was.

Paper Plates Please

Grandma and Grandpa were ready and waiting for us on the bench at the train station, sitting peacefully side by side with their overnight bags. They were, for once, alone. Usually they arrive toting one or more grandsons from Seattle in their camper van, a jolly crowd descending upon us. We'd requested they arrive solo, not because we don't love our nephews, but because we needed their help to get this party off the ground, if only for the moral support.

When we reached our house with a take-out lunch, the Maid Brigade women were still trying to find our kitchen countertop under the dirt, so we huddled around the coffee table in the upstairs playroom having lunch, hearing gossip, and bringing the grandparents up to speed on the agenda: I was putting Graeme down for a nap, the older children were going to be angels and play quietly, and they were going to Costco with Jannine to buy *lots* of food.

Grandma and Grandpa love Costco.

On the way, Jannine explained to her parents (in, I trust, a diplomatic fashion) that they were not to dirty a single dish, fork, or spoon before the wedding reception the following afternoon. We would be having take-out meals: paper plates only, plastic cutlery, paper napkins.

She knew (but didn't tell her parents) that I was a woman on the edge, severely sleep deprived, on emotional overload, up to my aching armpit in unused breast milk, and I couldn't handle normal wear and tear on top of prepping for a reception. Jannine didn't want dirty dishes to be the straw that broke the camel's back, sending me running to the store for beer and cigarettes, and never coming back; her parents, bless them, said OK, and happily ate off paper plates, scrupulously avoided non-disposable kitchen items, and in no way hindered our efforts to arrive at Sunday without a nervous breakdown.

Hours later, they returned from Costco with provisions for an army. It was good that Jannine was in charge of food procurement, she came back with things I'd never have thought of: smoked salmon, barbecued pork, cold cuts, crackers, and cream puffs, in simply enormous quantities. We enlisted the kids to carry in the bottled beverages, lining them up along the deck for the night to keep them cold.

Sunday morning arrived sunny and uncharacteristically warm. I managed to get up before the rest of the family, and stepped out to get the newspaper in my bare feet and pajamas. The galvanized bins were ready to fill with ice and drinks, the steps were decorated with flowering annuals, and the silver "Just Married" banner that Terri bought us was hung over our porch, announcing our news.

The newspaper was on the lower steps by the sidewalk, and as I reached for the paper, I saw the pile of dog poop directly in front of our bottom step.

I tried to imagine a scenario in which a dog owner would allow his dog to poop in front of someone's steps, and not at least clean it up, or pull the dog away mid-poop. I didn't like to think it was on purpose, but that pile was perfectly positioned.

I slipped the plastic bag off my Sunday *Oregonian* and picked up the dog debris, then started back across our lawn to the driveway and garbage cans. Three steps across the grass I saw it, the razor blade wedged blade up in the grass path, seemingly placed so that a barefoot adult or child walking from door to driveway might get sliced. I stooped, looked closer, and tried to wrap my mind around any other way it could have arrived there. Maybe it worked its way up through the soil, or fell when someone was walking across the grass, carrying, for some reason, an unwrapped razor blade?

I picked it up and dropped it with the bag of dog doo in our garbage can, grabbed my newspaper, and went back inside to read the comics and regain my Zen for the day.

It was a slow motion morning. Somehow, the rush was over. Everything that could be done was done. We'd cleared the decks as much as is possible when you have three kids and fifteen pets: one dog, two rabbits, two guinea pigs, five birds, two lizards, two frogs, and a fish; Maid Brigade had done their best, and now it was time to let it be. If it rained, we had no idea where we would put people, but if it didn't, we could open the front door and use the porch for overflow, the side deck could take another dozen, and the back steps four, in a pinch, though they were pretty rickety, and would later come down with a couple of blows from a sledgehammer one weekend morning when Jannine was feeling inspired.

Jannine got dressed in five minutes flat, as usual, in jeans and a Ward Cleaver shirt buttoned over a white T-shirt, after asking me, "Honey, what do you want me to wear?" I dressed the boys: Duncan in khakis and a jean shirt, Graeme in jeans and his cowboy shirt from our friend, Pam, a long-sleeve onesie with retro cowboys printed all over the fabric, and Anna dressed herself in the white lace T-shirt and black velvet skirt we bought in a speedy shopping excursion the Friday after our wedding. In consideration of my grotesquely lopsided condition, I wore my jean jacket over my black tank, thereby coordinating with our girl, both boys, and my wife!

I slipped on the black and white striped garter belt Terri bought for me during her visit to the party store, and was disturbed that it bit into my thigh, though I shrugged and kept it on for luck, figuring it was a sign that I needed to think about some exercise. Pulling it off hours later, and returning it to its package, I saw that Terri had accidentally bought an arm band, instead of a garter.

I brushed Anna's hair into an upswept, glossy blonde pony tail. We even had time to paint our toenails in what our friend Sheila calls "Hooker Red," and I gave her a kiss of lipstick and a brush of blush in honor of the day.

Everything seemed under control. The sun was shining. The children looked like angels. All was right in our world. No dog doo or razor blade could dampen the day.

Wishy-Washy Unitarians

At ten-thirty, we dragged Grandma off to church, leaving Grandpa to hold down the fort.

Typically, Jannine and I sit in "the baby room" during service, a cavernous basement room that soundproofs the congregation from squealing toddlers, ply Graeme with pretzels, and listen to the televised service, while the older two kids go to their Sunday school classrooms and learn about diverse beliefs, their Judeo/Christian heritage, play fruit basket upset with children of liberal parents, and eat graham crackers.

Jannine and I had a tug of war over our destination, she wanting to sit upstairs, me feeling like a fussy toddler wasn't worth any slim chance of success; we ended up downstairs. When the weekly announcements began, and the intern minister started to speak the names of the fifteen same-sex couples who were married in the church that week (the outside of the church was hung with a huge "Freedom to Marry" banner), Jannine scooped up Graeme, grabbed my hand and we made a mad dash for the sanctuary, to be there when our names were called.

The couples were asked to stand when their names were called, and we ran in, me skidding over the slippery doorway in my Cruella deVille shoes, just as the last syllables of Jannine's name were ending. We stood happily holding our last born child while the rest of the names were called out, the congregation applauding each set of newlyweds. When all the couples were named, the congregation gave us a standing ovation. We all could only beam, make eye contact with the other couples—who knew how much this meant, and cry a little at this overwhelming recognition and celebration of our unions.

In Chris's kindergarten classroom upstairs, where she was teaching Sunday school, Chris was treated to a standing ovation of cheering five year-olds.

Still buzzed by the warmth of the congregation, we went to the coffee hour in Fuller Hall after the service, and found it packed with congregants happily eating sheet cake in our collective honor. Jannine turned into a social butterfly, chatting up her fellow Sunday school parents, swapping stories with Tom, the Minister, while I baby-wrangled from the sidelines, glad to sidestep the limelight and save my energy for what was to come.

Despite Jannine ending up behind one of the tables cutting cake with Lisa, five years of episodic Sunday school attendance by our kids, and our eagerness for Associate Minister Tom Disrud to perform our desperately desired marriage, we are wishy-washy Unitarians.

My shaky relationship with any religion is grounded not only in my never-ending adolescent rebellion (that I should surely have outgrown), but in my strictly atheist upbringing; my father was a former Methodist who didn't believe in anything during my formative years, and told me that I should tell people I was a secular humanist; my mother was an atheist who found God as a teenager, lost faith, returned to atheism throughout my childhood, then found God again when I was already in my teens. Her resumption of religion terribly disappointed my maternal grandfather, because that made two of his three daughters who had joined religions—my aunt converted to Judaism after she was assured she didn't have to believe in God, just live a good Jewish life—when he'd tried so hard to raise them as good atheists.

Apparently, my mother's grandmother (daughter of the Victorian Beauty/wife of the stock market crash suicide/mother of my socialist grandmother) was an active and lifelong Unitarian who, after retiring, worked to promote civil rights during the sixties, though I was too young and clueless to learn about her work before she died at ninety-three.

Jannine is a lapsed-Lutheran; unable to shake her belief in God, even when she wanted to, which she did for a period when, having found me, she felt rejected by her religion. But even before that, despite religious education, regular attendance, and her parents' involvement, she'd never found it a spiritual home. It had seemed too much about fund-raising, proselytizing, being a bigger church, and bringing power to the pulpit, and too little about how to live a humane life in a world that God seemed to have increasingly abandoned.

We came to the First Unitarian Church not kicking and screaming, but dragging our feet. It took us years to realize that all of our lesbian mom friends were flocking there each Sunday, no one said a word. It was no one's doing but our own when we decided to give it a try, years ago, much to our children's dismay.

Unlike many, for whom Unitarian Universalism represents freedom from oppressive dogma and a less structured religion, to the un-churched, it can seem darned traditional. First Unitarian Church is particularly full of its Christian and Jewish roots: the handing round of the plate, the focus on fund raising (even a

Catholic emphasis on tithing), the singing of hymns, the annual Christmas pageant, and a strangely constant use of the word "God" when I am assured that questioning the existence of a deity is the norm. Sometimes, I feel like I'm missing something I should have learned in Church 101, when I was busy contemplating my navel, but then, if Church 101 was required for attendance, they'd have lost me.

Yet it was I who pushed our family to church. I am a spiritual nomad, incapable of any faith but the faith you must have to raise children or fall in love. I know that the liberal parents, little old ladies, and Generation X upstarts who make up the congregation struggle with issues that we share: how do we not only oppose war, but do what it takes to make peace? How do we live a just life in an unjust society? How do we remain conscious of the struggles of the world, yet maintain joy? Is faith really required, or can ethical living be a religion?

What keeps us Unitarians (in our wishy-washy way) is not the popular oration of Senior Minister Marilyn Sewell, or even the humble homilies of Tom, but the open hearts of the congregation who stood up for us to celebrate our marriages, applauding sincerely our victory, and love. One of the consistent messages of the church is a respect for diversity that is not tolerance of gays and lesbians, but acceptance of all people as equal and worthy.

Which is why we chose to get married in the First Church; even on those days when we aren't sure that it is our spiritual home, it is always a community that welcomes us, doubts and all, and where we know that we belong.

The Cake Arrives Without Us

The reception was a mosh pit leap of faith for us. We threw our announcement to the wind, did what we could, farmed out the rest, taking people up on any and all offers of aid, and trusted that our friends and family would come through. They did.

Laurie arrived at our front door just after we left for church, with two enormous and fragrant bouquets made up of flowers I didn't know existed, and stayed on to assist with food, prep, and any friction that might occur between mothers, aunts, or arriving relatives.

Laurie is a "people person" with enviable social skills (as well as that enviable wardrobe) who manages to be simultaneously bubbly and coolly efficient. She is lovely, willowy, and recently single, though when we met nine years ago at the co-op preschool, she was managing to be lovely and willowy, while pregnant with her daughter, Elia, and was married to Matt, who is a nice guy, a good dad, and since cutting off his long hair, bears an uncanny resemblance to my father circa 1962 (chinos, horn rim glasses, slicked back dark hair, sideburns, not the strongest of chins). Their son, Kade, is a smooth operator who's been friends with Duncan since preschool, when Kade would routinely fall into a swoon dressed as Prince Charming in order to impress the girls, when he wasn't challenging someone to a duel. He greeted the news of our marriage with a whoop and a cheer and an "All Right!" while his eight year-old sister, Elia, responded in the way so many children did upon hearing the news.

"I thought they were already married."

Aunt Maureen arrived in a whirlwind of crystal dishes, sterling silver trays, and lace table cloths that elevated our event to a whole new level, beyond Costco, and darned near semi-formal. She dove right into setting out the food, arranging tasty homemade canapés in circles, and moving Costco veggies onto more suitable display.

While we were cutting cake in Fuller Hall, my mother and her sister, Maggie, arrived at our house bearing baklava, pita bread, and hummus. Maggie drove down from Everett, Washington, the day before, having been called into action on behalf of my side of the family, fortunately available on a moment's notice.

There are three sisters in that generation, the daughters of David and Elaine, who had been socialists, intellectuals, conscientious objectors, and atheists, and put away an astounding amount of vodka, though they always waited until cocktail hour, and were not atypical of their milieu re: such habits. My grandmother, who went by Mima, blessed our relationship early on when she said she "saw waves" between us, illustrating this with a dramatic arm gesture and almost a wink. My grandfather looked on Jannine as a son-in-law of sorts, and a favorite one at that.

My Aunt Maggie is the blonde in the trio of sisters, a vivacious middle child who attracts men in droves. My mother is the brunette, the eldest of the girls, intellectual, shy, and done, thoroughly done, with men. My Aunt Miranda is the redhead, younger by several years, and still deep in the trenches of childrearing.

It is strangely ironic that the women who helped most in making the celebration of our wedding possible are themselves single and divorced.

Our buddy Jason (also single, though never married) arrived with the wedding cake while we were gone. It was perfect: two-tiered, white, traditional, and elegant. Everything I would have asked for, if I'd been asked.

I was not, in an unspoken understanding with my wife, being asked for too many particulars during the days preceding this event, which left a lot up to Jannine.

When our friend Jason called with an earnest desire to order us a wedding cake, Jannine initially told him "No," but then called him back, and asked if he was serious. He was. She gave him four pieces of information: when, where, approximate number of guests, and to keep it traditional.

When we thanked him again and again later, he told us to stop, "It made my week!" Apparently, he had gone to the bakery, Helen Bernhard's, and asked to see the wedding cake book with photographs of all the various designs, options, and prices. He and the bakery assistant started looking through it, beginning with the very traditional white, tiered cakes, and moved toward the unconventional. When he told her that it was a lesbian wedding, she said, "Oh!" and opened the book to the rainbow section. Jason told us he said, "Oh, no," grabbed the book back out of her hand, and flipped right back to the traditional cakes. He knows us well.

With the cake, Jason brought a porcelain wedding topper of two women in white dresses with actual veils that can be flipped back and forth like bridal action figures. They came from a company that makes mix-and-match wedding figures that come in a choice of genders and ethnicities. You can have an Asian man and an African-American woman. You can have a white man and a Hispanic woman.

You can have an African-American man and a white man. Or, in this case, two white women. The clerk told Jason he'd made a mistake when he brought them to the checkout, drawing his attention to the fact that they were both female, and Jason said, "Where have you been all week? Haven't you seen the news?"

Maureen and Laurie arranged the table in our dining room bay window, the wedding cake taking center stage, flanked by flowers and food. Everything was ready.

The Street Where We Live

As we pulled up to the curb near our house, Jannine saw Graeme close his eyes and fall asleep, in the rearview mirror. We sat there, considering our options, while the March sun illuminated a neighborhood bursting into spring.

We live in a nice, cozy, liberal enclave of Portland. The homes look like illustrations lifted from the *Dick and Jane* books we grew up on as first readers, before the days of "whole language" and "creative spelling." The houses have white picket fences or smooth grass fronts kept that way by lawn care experts and expensive organic treatments done discreetly while the neighbors are at work. The doors are painted red, and the flowers seemingly always in bloom. The cars are different from *Dick and Jane*; instead of a station wagon in every garage, a sea of mint green minivans and muted gold SUVs line the streets and fill the driveways, the garages too full of bicycles, exercise equipment, and over-flowing outdoor gear to allow vehicular habitation.

When we first moved here, after a harrowing real estate purchase involving our real estate agent (who I came to fear) and the sellers' real estate agent (who saved our bacon) I could hardly believe it was true, we were living in La-La Land. The houses are Hollywood pretty, and belong in the *Father of the Bride* movies, though it was *Mr. Holland's Opus* that was filmed around the corner at Grant High, one block away. The house at the end of our street is referred to as "The K-Mart House" because a K-Mart Christmas commercial was filmed there several years ago, and every summer a couple nearby streets are blocked with trailers, trucks, equipment, and gawkers, as another director finishes shooting a feature film.

Not that our house belongs in anything but a feature on "do-it-yourself house projects gone bad." The asbestos siding is broken in places, the paint could use a touch up (though our ebullient greenery covers most flaws), but to us, it is paradise, and we feel no pressure to hire lawn experts or add on a wing.

This house is a huge step up from our previous dwellings. Before this, we owned a house in Tacoma for which we have warm and nostalgic feelings, both of us drawn to houses resembling it: tall salt boxes with big windows on either side of the front door and asbestos siding. We lived there for only ten months.

We bought it shortly after Duncan was born, sure that as parents we should provide him with a backyard, a picket fence, and maybe a dog. We were, however, suddenly living on a single income (when Duncan was born and placed, warm and purple, on my naked belly, I turned to Jannine and said, "I'm not going back to work," and she said, "I know."), and we needed to buy somewhere we could afford, which turned out to be Tacoma.

Our real estate agent was the mother of a friend, and she painted a lovely picture of the neighborhood, its history, its varied architecture, its nearness to schools and stores. During initial visits to the house, which had wood floors, yellow walls, and a large yard, it seemed like a "grandma house," just right for our vintage furniture and garage sale lifestyle. We didn't know that we would have a chained-up attack dog on one side, and a crack-addicted mother of three teenage boys on the other, as soon as the deal closed.

Four doors down from that house was a young man with schizophrenia who would go off his medication, hear God telling him to quit drinking and using cocaine, prompting him to saw off his arm and nose one night with a serrated bread knife. A neighbor heard thumping on the outside wall of her house and found the man's bleeding, unconscious body spread-eagled on her lawn when she opened her door. In a feat of medical legerdemain, surgeons managed to reattach his nose and arm after he was airlifted via helicopter to Harborview Hospital.

Prior to that, we lived in that condominium in Kent with a stand on your tippy-toes view of Puget Sound from our living room, and a close proximity to Pacific Highway, known for its strip malls, fast food restaurants, and as the hunting ground for the Green River Killer. It had ugly carpeting, an even uglier fireplace, and was smaller than our previous apartment. We were proud as punch. It was ours.

Of course, when we first lived together, we were just out of college and had nothing. Our first apartment overlooked a gas station at the intersection of Pike Street and Broadway on Capitol Hill, in Seattle. The gay bar to the west pounded music into the wee hours. If you leaned out the bay window, you could see the line of motorcycles in front of The Wild Rose lesbian tavern to the east. The apartment had cockroaches and mice, and my purse was stolen while I was moving into the building. But it was a good place to be young, gay, single, and poor, which I was when I moved in.

Being not so young, still gay, happily married, and middle class, we are thrilled to live in our neighborhood, and don't intend to leave it any way except feet first.

There is more to like about it than the architecture and the sense that if you had to walk to the store after dark, it wouldn't be a life threatening situation. This is a seriously liberal neighborhood. This may have to do with education and socio-economics, but I think it also has to do with values. You see a lot of organic vegetables being delivered here. You can't throw a rock without hitting a stay-at-home mom or a green space. And on recycling days, the homeless men come for miles to get the curbside pickings as every can, bottle, and paper product is rinsed, bagged, sorted by type, and turned into something other than landfill.

These are the kind of Portlanders who helped defeat the host of anti-gay measures that the Oregon Citizens Alliance has tried to foist on us over the years, the voters who had to make up their minds about what they really thought about gay people, and whether we had rights, too. And overwhelmingly, they believed we did.

These are the people in our neighborhood.

Relative City Comes to Us

There was a party happening at our house, and we weren't even there. From the front seats of our minivan we could see Jannine's brother, Erik, setting out beverages on our front porch. Aunt Maureen was putting a wide pot of flowering annuals on the front steps with her son, Russell, and his family. Cousin Tom, who lives up to his nickname "Moose," was parking his truck. We were suddenly nervous.

Graeme defied all expectations by staying asleep during the walk into the house (he normally wakes like a shot if anything is going on), during which we greeted relatives, gave hugs, and exchanged kisses with kin. Astoundingly, he remained asleep during a transfer to Grandpa's arms, where he spent the first hour of our reception, sleeping like the proverbial baby.

I didn't know what to do with all the freedom to mingle and use both hands, and Grandpa had the ideal excuse to lounge on the couch in a semi-prone position. Several people offered to take Graeme off his hands, but he jealously guarded his opportunity to snuggle a sleeping little guy.

All the other grandkids were getting big.

Jannine got busy dumping more ice into the metal tubs, digging out the Costco offerings that had yet to be unearthed, and finding the gross of paper napkins we'd stored in the basement, after she'd made appreciative noises over the cake, greeted my mother, hugged the rest of the assorted arrivals, and thanked Laurie for the beautiful flowers.

The party had barely begun when Jannine's three aunts: Bunny, Gayle, and Paula, walked in the door after the three hour drive from Eastern Washington. They came bearing gifts and Jannine's cousin, Ally, a year younger than Anna. Ally quickly located Anna, who took her upstairs to the kid zone, while Bunny and Paula cornered Grandma in the kitchen for a rare opportunity to catch up on the latest family gossip. These two aunts would face the three hour drive again that night, while Gayle stayed on to visit with her sons, Eric and Tom, who were standing in the kitchen trying to guess the age of our pink double-stove from the fifties known as Big Pink.

Jannine's aunts are feisty, fun, and tough as nails. Thirteen years ago, when her three teenage boys questioned her about how I'd managed to get pregnant (and be a lesbian), Gayle explained, "They A.I.'d her, like the cows." They said, "Oh, OK," and were good to go, since they knew all about bull semen, and mentally adjusted the mechanics. Since then, we've seen this side of the family regularly, attending the weddings of all three of Gayle's sons, and getting the chance to help a little when Gayle's husband, Carl, went through chemotherapy before succumbing to cancer over three years ago.

Gayle and Carl taught us a lot about being in a family, and raising one. They have been part of our life together ever since that first Thanksgiving I spent with Jannine's folks, which coincided with a rare visit from Gayle and family. Their son, Eric, sat wedged in next to me, a fourteen year-old wise man, and while passing the potatoes gave me the wink that he *knew*, even though at that time I was allegedly "just a friend."

Years later, when I was insanely pregnant with Anna, and feeling huge, harried, and overwhelmed, we went for dinner at their house. I looked at Gayle and Carl's long kitchen table, where they had fed scores of their boys' friends over the years, supervised homework, and worked through the tough times, and saw that it could be done; family life with multiple kids could work.

Their sons helped us move into our house. Carl came out and supervised, making sure his teenage boys earned the modest amount we paid them. Carl was a tough guy, but a gentleman.

It was never an issue, our being lesbians. We were just folks, like them, trying to raise good kids. Carl treated me like a lady, which is a stretch, and Jannine like one of the boys, which isn't. Even in her teens, he was an influence, taking her on her first motorcycle ride, kick-starting her love affair with speed on sunny afternoons.

It was in May, when out of the blue, he had a seizure and doctors discovered the brain tumors, and the lung cancer, and the rest. He didn't feel sick. He didn't believe it could be true. How could someone who felt so good have six months to live?

He came to Portland for treatment, and we were able to offer Gayle and Carl the use of our basement apartment for as long as they needed it.

It was really only a couple of weeks in all, but hard ones for them. Carl became sick with the radiation and never really bounced back. I tried not to hover or interfere, worried that I wasn't doing enough. It was only when they were getting ready to go back home that Carl talked about his seclusion. He was feeling better that day, chatty, and while the kids were rolling on the floor talking to Gayle, he turned to me. He said he was sorry he hadn't seen us more, but that the radiation affected his moods, and he didn't know if he could hold it together in front of the kids, that he might say something ... He didn't want to do that. He had tears in his eyes, the cancer taking away all the emotional filters we use to keep our vulnerability at bay. At his most vulnerable, he was thinking of others.

He'd have gotten a kick out of our reception.

It seems to be weddings, funerals, and baby showers that bring family together. It was our baby shower that opened the door to the Eastern Washington branch. Before Duncan, Jannine's mom was so concerned with our remaining closeted that when we bought the condo, she told us we'd have a bed in our spare room if she had to carry one there on her back. She was only partially kidding.

When we got pregnant with Duncan, Jannine called her grandma. Back then, all I knew was that they were from a small town, that Jannine's grandpa had been a prisoner of war during World War Two, and that he thought the military was the best thing that ever happened to him. I put two and two together and made seventeen, molding him into some kind of right wing bogeyman.

When Jannine called her grandma and told her, "Maybe you should sit down," I didn't know how it would go.

Jannine started with, "Grandma, I'm gay.'

"We knew that, honey," her grandma responded immediately, her voice warm.

"There's more," Jannine went on, "We're having a baby. Beren is pregnant and we're having a baby shower in two weeks and we wanted you to come."

There was a pause.

"Well, of course, I'd be delighted," her grandma said, and they finished the call with mutual assurance of affection. A minute later, the phone rang. It was Jannine's grandma again.

"Can I tell your aunts? They'll want to come, too."

At the baby shower, Jannine's grandfather greeted me with a hug, thanked me for bringing new family members into the fold, and told me, "You're doing a good job," which, bless his heart, he does every time he sees me, something every mother needs to hear. Far from a right wing bogeyman, he is an ultra-liberal who argues politics with his cronies at the coffee shop every morning, doing his part to open minds and spur debate.

Years later, Jannine would joke with him (while I was pregnant with number three) that she must not have been shooting blanks after all, which gave him a chuckle. Though after Graeme was in the world, and a carbon copy of numbers one and two, her Uncle Max joked back that at least when I was stepping out on her, it wasn't very often and was with the same guy.

The Reception of Love

The kids played upstairs, but came down frequently for food and drink, and to make sure they weren't missing anything. Thinking in advance, we offered Duncan five bucks to keep the peace and ensure the upstairs didn't become a disaster zone, or any of the kids get hurt. He did a good job, and without having to become a drill sergeant.

Though he spent the first part of the party telling various adults that we had President Bush to thank for our opportunity to marry, theorizing that Bush had so inflamed the elected officials of the county by his blatant prejudice that they were spurred to take action, and that Bush was making it obvious how wrong a ban on same-sex marriage was.

Dozens of friends came, some dressed up, and others dressed down, most of them with one day's notice. The mood was exultant. My Aunt Maggie said afterward that it was an incredible group of people. They were thrilled we could get married. Over and over, we were told by friends that when they'd heard about Multnomah County granting marriage licenses to same-sex couples, they'd thought of us. Jannine's self-described "red neck" cousin Tom, a man famous for his hazardous firework techniques, frequent injuries, and resemblance in size to a refrigerator, told us he didn't think there were two people more meant to be married than we were.

Our neighbor, John, whose wife, Carol, was one of the first to call after the happy event, said he was thrilled for us.

John seems like an unlikely proponent of same-sex marriage. He is ex-military, a Boy Scout leader, probably a member of the NRA, and the same age as Jannine's father, someone it would be easy to jump to conclusions about. He stood in our living room telling me how he and other leaders in the local scouting community were pushing to end what he called "the ridiculous" ban on gay participation in scouting. He was appalled at the prejudice and ignorance of the national policy. He told me he and others were working on making change from within.

Their fourteen year-old son, Thad, has spent time with us on almost every Christmas morning for a decade, confused in the early days at the strange lack of sports equipment in the haul, a Santa Clausal inequity he could barely fathom.

Their daughter, Xan, was the first babysitter we trusted with our offspring, and Anna still has the bottle of sprinkle glitter she gave her for Christmas one year, to stop a three year-old Anna from raiding her own.

Duncan's earliest childhood friend was touring the upstairs with her family. They'd been our first friends here, and their older daughter, Blayke, his first playmate, before they moved a decade ago. They'd recently returned to Portland with their younger daughter, Beren, as well, and were checking out the changes in our house, which, when they'd seen it last, had pink wall-to-wall carpeting downstairs, patchwork carpet upstairs, and blue bathrooms on both floors that made us wince.

Duncan's fourth and fifth grade teachers, Diane and Chris, came giddily in the door, bearing a joint wedding present: Diane, a no-nonsense Brooklynite capable of tough love in the classroom, and Chris, a stylish character out of a picture book hybrid of *Madeline* and *Eloise* who never knew a fifth grader she didn't like. They were beaming.

There is something vulnerable about having your kid's teachers in your house, as if they have a window into your world they didn't before, or as if suddenly you are the child again, and they, the adults. Though these women are more than good teachers, they are good friends.

Diane told us she doesn't get this whole opposition to same-sex marriage thing. She and Chris both reiterated, if we're good parents, who cares what gender we are? That's what really counts. Why shouldn't we get married?

Before we had kids, school had been one of our most constant concerns. Would they be teased? Would their teachers support them? Would the school accept and support our family? Twelve years into lesbian parenting, so far so good. I interviewed our vice-principal for an article last year, and he thought gay and lesbian parents were simply no big deal anymore.

Anna's guitar teacher, Dan, and his family came, thrilled that our county did something right for a change. He and his wife, Fran, are frighteningly well-informed, and were as excited about this local example of equality as any same-sex couple could be.

Out on the deck were four-fifths of the Manzi clan, an east coast family who have pointed out to us frequently that same-sex couples aren't the only ones to face difficulties when they fall in love, and assure us that combining an Irish Catholic woman with an Italian Catholic man can be just as problematic in the in-law department as any lesbian couple might encounter. But they agree that it's ridiculous for us not to be able to marry (if they can), and are proud to be from Massachusetts, where marriage for same-sex partners was then imminent.

We got to know them when our exuberant and verbose sons became friends, despite the fact that their fear philosophies are in exact opposition to ours, and we've decided it will be at their house that our children will break their arms for the first time. They openly mock my safety queen status, and gleefully point out any ways that I allow potential harm into our children's lives ("Look, nail polish remover! Why aren't those table corners covered? Do you have combination locks on your poison cupboard?"), while assuring us that Graeme, as a third child, is protected by his very own guardian angel.

We had more people in our living room, our kitchen, and spilling onto our deck and front porch than we'd ever had before, and, as lesbians of a certain age, we've had some pretty big potlucks. Many of these friends are parents like us, trying to raise their kids the best way they can. We feel lucky to know them, amazed to think that ten years before, we hardly knew anyone in Portland.

When We First Came to Portland

One of the most challenging things about being a stay-at-home mom is the isolation. When our older kids were young, I was around people all day, but they'd either be talking a blue streak about dinosaurs, handing me a pile of books to read, or needing a diaper change. I was never alone, but often lonely, while up to my elbows in dishes or indescribable body fluids.

At times, I've wished for co-workers. They allow you to obsess about your job to a degree that simply won't be tolerated by others not in the field. When I start telling Jannine about the sub-context in a Disney film, or ask her whether she's noticed the preponderance of divorce in kids' movies, her eyes glaze over and I lose her. But when I talk to another stay-at-home parent about the same thing, he or she understands, has seen the film under discussion twenty times or more during the eleven-month flu season, and has analyzed the hell out of it, too.

Though finding moms you can talk to about compulsory heterosexuality in juvenile entertainment is harder. Stay-at-home moms you can find, lesbian ones are few and far between. Though, since it seems every lesbian couple in America is spawning, the odds are increasing.

In those early days in Portland, when I spied a mom, straight or gay, who looked like a potential comrade, we did the mommy-dance. It's not unlike the way dogs circle each other when they first meet. The mommy-dance consists of manipulating your children into either moving towards the area where the other mom's children are playing or stalling your children while she moves to you. The second phase of the dance consists of remarks which reveal the depth of your parenting commitment. One might open with, "Did you notice the glass near the slide?" The other mom will respond with, "One day, I was here and someone had peed in the tunnel," which will lead almost inevitably to a discussion of AIDS, gangs, child abuse, the state of the schools today, the hole in the ozone layer, random violence, commercial television, kidnapping, and belly button rings. By the end of ten minutes, or when your children are ready to drag you away by your hair, you've catalogued each others' fears and decided whether they are compatible and you can be friends.

So much of early parenting is about keeping your children out of harm's way while they have the common sense of a flea.

Phase three involves more sharing of fear, can go on for years, and evolves over time to the kvetching parents do about their kid's messy room, questionable grades, or frightening dating choices. My friend, Amy, and I used to get together and carry on under a cloud of life-threatening gloom and doom for hours. It was like knocking wood. You think if you catalogue every horrible thing that can befall your children, then it won't be able to sneak up on you unawares.

We found a lot of these friends in our house, spilling out on the porch, or dissing President Bush on the deck, during times of worry. Shared interests or values kept us in touch past whatever crisis brought us together, so that by the time they came to celebrate our marriage with us, there was absolutely no gloom and doom to be seen.

However, I did find myself standing on our deck in the sunshine, holding a Diet Coke and chatting merrily to Megan, my mother, and Aunt Maggie in a rapt state of marital bliss about the eventuality of civil unions, saying that they were better than a kick in the head. At my own wedding reception, I was talking about accepting this second class solution with a smile. It must have been the sleep deprivation.

Ironically, Megan and the others were ticked off that this option should be presented by anyone as an acceptable alternative. "It should be marriage!" Megan insisted. They were mad for us that we should live in a country that would even consider passing a constitutional amendment to make sure we cannot marry, as Bush was proposing, and would offer us civil unions to keep the liberals happy and us firmly in our place.

My mother insisted, "I think your marriage will stand. The state won't be able to take it away. It's hard to undo something that has been done," reiterating the sentiment Thad, John and Carol's teenage son, had expressed about the Multnomah County marriages, "You can't get the toothpaste back in, once it's out of the tube."

Soon there were cries of "Cake, cake, cut the cake!" and Jannine and I were ushered to where the dining table had been pulled out, so that we could enjoy the traditional cake cutting ritual.

The kids, who had been invisible throughout most of the party, suddenly appeared like vultures when the cry of "Cake!" rippled through the house, and there were paper plates held out eagerly as we joined hands to slice through the top layer. It was a sight, all those excited young people, most of them assuming we were already married before that Wednesday morning, in happy ignorance of the law. We loaded up the kids with cake; then Grandma took over to dish out slices, while we had some of the best wedding cake we've ever eaten, all the sweeter due to the day.

The Inevitable Question

Sometime, in the light of all this, someone is going to ask us "the question" again. Do you want your kids to be gay?

It's come up plenty over the years. It's the universal question gay and lesbian parents get asked, and not just by straight folks. It comes somewhere after, "Where did you get your son and/or daughter?" and "Who gave birth?" Assumptions vary. Some assume we would do anything to prevent our child from suffering the same fate that makes us a member of a persecuted minority, the very timbre of their voices implying how cruel it would be to wish this upon a child. Others assume that if we took on parenting as a gay man or lesbian, we did it to perpetuate the species, and intend to mold, cajole, or genetically influence our kids' orientational outcome.

Both assumptions blow my mind.

But not the minds of other parents I've heard answer this question over the years. We were privy to one of these conversations awhile back, and when the lesbian mom involved was asked "the question," she made it clear she didn't want her son to be gay, that it would be more difficult, that she wouldn't have grandbabies, and that it wasn't "normal."

She didn't beat around the bush.

This is a response I've heard echoed over the years. Often, gay parents will say they'd have things easier for their children. Sometimes, they have suffered from homophobia almost beyond endurance, been rejected by family and friends, or experienced hate crimes, and one can understand their desire for something easier for their child.

Other times, I've heard responses that practically affirmed the old recruitment propaganda right wing America used to publish as truth. To these parents, being gay is a culture; they are raising their child in that culture, and they would like them to become full members in standing when they reach adulthood. They are happily living in a gay bubble surrounded by those like them, and hope for the same for their children.

We all want what's best for our children, but *best* comes in many guises.

With the new emphasis on genetics in childrearing and bioengineering the "perfect" child, people are bolder about this kind of question, as if tomorrow one could choose to have a gay or non-gay child at will. The assumption being that since the majority of parents would choose non-gay there is a responsibility to purposefully breed some potentially gay adults.

Though as my wife's straight surgeon said, when the topic came up regarding her new baby girl's eventual orientation, "That's the least of my worries." She was more worried about drugs, illness, and violence. Whether or not her daughter will be gay was just not a blip on her radar.

As parents, we are in neither camp, pro-gay or anti-gay. I'd like to say that I was purely and uncomplicatedly sure that I just want them to be who they are, solid, strong, gay, straight, or in-between, with no prejudice either way and happy at either outcome.

It's not that simple. While the goal is healthy, happy self-hood, whoever that may turn out to be, I have fears for that self, gay or straight. For my daughter, I have preconceived notions of heterosexual dating based on my experiences in high school. I can't erase that memory, and send her out into the hands of sixteen year-old boys someday without fear. Nor would I be carefree should my beautiful blonde sons come out as teenagers, knowing that a trip through the gay subculture is *de rigueur* and that the standards of appearance, the emphasis on sex and partying, and the objectification of young men would be a rough river to navigate safely and find healthy purchase on the other side.

That doesn't mean that I will greet our daughter's date at the door with a shotgun, or attempt to "scare straight" a gay adolescent, but I can't help but worry. Both sets of fears indicate preconceptions and prejudice, even internalized homophobia, but they are inside me, and I cannot change that, though I can certainly choose what I do with it.

Including understanding that it is not about me, it is about them, and their right to a happy, whole life, wherever that life takes them.

Thank You Everyone

Friends hung around until the end, eating up the sushi, nearly finishing the cake. Terri and Marty dragged McKenzie away around five o'clock. Terri had been our official photographer. At one point, we lined up all the relatives on our front porch: cousins, aunts, grandparents, siblings, plus Jeanna and Ellen's daughter, Jordyn, who didn't realize it was a family photo. It was a huge crowd standing on our front steps who'd managed to show up with two days' notice.

Through it all, our marriage license hung on the wall. Our friends, Liz and Nan, had it framed as a wedding present, just in time for the reception. Jannine had set up a revolving slide show on her laptop with pictures of the wait in line, the licensing office, and our wedding, as much of it as we had documented. She put it together knowing that with something this spontaneous, this unexpected, it wouldn't be real to people unless they could see it for themselves. Even for us, it was an amazing, unbelievable, ephemeral event we knew we would have to work to hold onto, legally and emotionally. Who'd have thought we'd see this day?

Despite there being two mothers- and one father-of-the-bride, none of them took the opportunity to throw a diva fit and demand things done his or her way. If they had any opinions about the way we went about the reception, or decorated, or did our hair (I ironed mine for the occasion), they kept it to themselves. Jannine's dad was just happy to help out, hang with Graeme, and chat with Marty, who is a walking cornucopia of useful and obscure facts. Grandma had sequestered herself with Auntie Maureen in the kitchen at one point and caught her up on how the other grandchildren were faring, the upcoming Union strike that would affect Jannine's sister, Cristy, and the latest work she'd been doing to the house. My mother kept close to Aunt Maggie, chatting up the guests, and having a long conversation about international travel with Jason's roommate, Christopher, who'd recently returned from Malaysia.

When all the guests and relatives had gone, filled with cake and our gratitude, our friends, Amy and Brian, stayed behind with their daughter, Jessica. They were crashing for the night, and then leaving at the crack of dawn to go back to Seattle.

I have known Amy since sophomore year in high school, when we wore a lot of eye make-up, dated a lot of boys, and wore white jeans—even more appalling than the boys. We are far from the girls who used to hang out in the halls of Lincoln High after school with Terri, who came out of the closet when he was fifteen. Terri is dead. Amy is a twice-divorced mother of two. I am a newly married, lesbian mother of three.

Our spouses were busily planning a cupboard they wanted to build together during a longer visit, and had begun to pull out power tools, while I opened wedding presents at the kitchen table with Amy and ate leftovers—I'd forgotten to eat all day—until the older kids put themselves to bed, and Graeme could stand it no more, and demanded to go to sleep—with me.

As I lay there in the darkness, the door to the kitchen closed to Jannine and Brian's dialogue on power saws, and miter boxes, and God only knows, the snores of our two older kids came from the foot of the bed and the alcove under the stairs where they'd bedded down for the night since their rooms were otherwise occupied. Graeme had gone down in minutes, his head nodding over book number two, and by book number three, he was out cold, his pink lips parted, his rosy cheeks warm and soft.

We'd done it. They were happy for us: our friends, our family, the people who mattered to us most in the world. The wedding and celebration we thought would never happen because it wouldn't be real, or legal, had happened. With a little help from our friends, we had pulled it off. It had been a labor of love.

Thank you, world.

Do You Feel Any Different?

"So how's married life treating you?"

It was a regular refrain in the days after our wedding, usually followed by, "Has getting married changed your relationship?" Traditional post-nuptial questions we'd never had the opportunity to experience before.

Some were just joking, moms at school taking the opportunity to rib us, dads getting to talk about our relationship in a playful way, which they might have felt was off-limits before. But some were deadly serious, as if suddenly, after seventeen years, we were more married than before. I realized that for them, saying "I do" was a distinct dividing line between the days before, and those that followed, in their own relationships.

Despite not having the chance to say "I do" all these years, we'd made the decisions that married people make every day: will I work to make this marriage succeed? Will I love you tomorrow, next week, next year, and in fifty years? Can we make it through this tough day as friends?

When asked, I replied that the relationship is the same. The love is the same. The commitment to working through troubles and staying together is the same. But, to more intimate friends, I admitted that it does feel different after saying the vows aloud.

I now understand why marriage vows are imbued with such ceremony. They do mean something beyond the words. Being asked, in a formal way, to state my feelings made me see my love for Jannine for what it was. Not just the everyday love that kisses goodbye in the morning, or snatches intimacy between sleepless nights and the latest birthday spectacular, but the *something more* that lies beneath. When I fell head over heels in love with her all those years ago, it stuck.

Luckily, we grew together—morally, ethically, in our vision of a life together—rather than apart. We are not the perfect couple, but we are good together. I was surprised and delighted to discover how much I love her, and to feel the same kind of love in return.

The kids feel different since our wedding.

Duncan has become the unofficial observer of gay and lesbian relationships wherever he goes, commenting when he sees a possible gay couple, in life or in the movies. He theorizes about the partnership of Timon and Pumba in *The Lion King 1½*, saying they are gay fathers because they sleep in the same bed and adopted Simba. He noticed the lesbian in *Mona Lisa Smile*, and agreed with me that the two male rhinoceroses in *Ice Age* are definitely a couple. He told me that he thinks the increase of gay characters in children's movies is a good sign.

He enjoyed his middle school teacher coming up for a hug after she'd seen us on television, the woman in the school office smiling when she saw his note excusing his absence, and loves to tell the story about waiting in line to get our marriage license: the donuts, the protesters, the wall-to-wall reporters.

But, he was also harassed for having lesbian moms, for the first time. He was at a new school. He hadn't known the kids since kindergarten. They had no long-term loyalty to him or to his family, and they were middle schoolers, full of the cruelty of their kind. He heard crude remarks about how we conceived him, was asked if we "make out and stuff," and was treated to explicit sexual comments about his mothers. He told us, when we asked how he dealt with it, that he stayed cool, disappointing his would-be tormentors who were trying to get a rise out of him.

Jannine suggested that there was a time and place to just go ahead and slug someone.

The publicity around our wedding has also shown him that there are kids at his school who support our family. One girl in class has been extra friendly since she found out about his two moms, and even one of his tormentors chimed in during a group discussion on the mechanics of Duncan and his siblings' conception, saying that we'd "gone and bought sperm from a sperm bank," and I wondered if maybe, with all the attention on same-sex marriage, there had been discussions in that kid's home that were changing his attitudes, too.

When his health class required a persuasive essay, Duncan chose to write his about same-sex marriage. His core argument being that same-sex marriage harmed no one, and made gay couples happy, and wasn't more happiness in the world a good thing?

Anna admitted after we married that she had always just thought we were married, even though she knew intellectually that we weren't. Her gay-friendly bubble wasn't burst at our elementary school packed with liberal parents and their kids. Not only did her teacher, Mr. McElroy, high-five her and give us all a hug, the secretary in the school office practically broadcast the news on that amazing Wednesday morning. It was all over the school.

When our kids were younger, if they asked if we were married, we'd tell them, "Well ..." explaining that legally we weren't, but in every other sense of the word, we were. We considered ourselves married, explained about our rings, and the nature of a marriage commitment. We hope Graeme will grow up without the, "Well ..."

For his whole life, he will know the story of how his parents went down to the County Building when he was one, and were married with him in their arms. Whether the courts let it stand is another issue. We got married. He can look at marriage photos, finger the wedding gifts around our home, read in newspaper clippings about the day his parents exchanged vows, and see our license on the wall. He is, I hope, just the beginning of a generation of kids whose gay parents will be married.

I know that for some asking, "How is married life treating you?" our marriage seemed unreal, because it was over in a moment and without the blessing of the voters. Local newspaper columnists wallowed in the idea that haste makes a marriage somehow distasteful, as if we were all shotgun brides or grooms, slipping through a window we had no business using. We, ourselves, joked that it was a shotgun wedding, but instead of being a baby on the way, it was an injunction.

Today, we know that we could have waited a couple weeks, invited people from near and far, made up a list, and ordered a dress. But, we'd have worried every minute that we'd made the wrong decision, that we'd waited too long, would miss this opportunity, then have to wait weeks, months, or even years for the window to open again. It would have been devastating.

One Month Later

One month into same-sex marriage in Multnomah County (the only place in the United States still issuing marriage licenses for same-sex couples after a spate of ceremonies in San Francisco, upstate New York, and New Mexico), we were still getting flowers on our front porch.

Even as the Multnomah County Commissioners revisited their decision to grant marriage licenses to same-sex couples, reviewed the procedure, held three town hall public discussions in which a narrow margin of supporters outweighed those against the marriages, only to vote again in favor of granting licenses to same-sex couples, we received more congratulatory cards in the mail, including one from Duncan's preschool teacher, who, bless her heart, told her class, "Yes, boys can marry boys," when the issue came up a decade ago in her classroom.

The weekend after that, we came home to tulips from a family we've known since those same preschool days (when our computer gaming sons were small and lacked facial hair), who'd heard about our wedding because of an interview we gave in the *Willamette Week,* a hip, provocative periodical aimed at the permanently cool, for their regular marriage column "Hitched."

It was strange to be interviewed, and I paced anxiously through the house awaiting the reporter's arrival, though I became significantly less intimidated when she showed up in a retro polyester dress and horn rim glasses, and was ten years our junior.

Being immersed in childrearing and the minutiae of daily life, I'm unpracticed at talking on non-domestic topics (I do better in print than in person), but Jannine was ready. As she's retold the story of her stay in line overnight, she has become firmer about her feelings regarding same-sex marriage, becoming uncharacteristically political and outspoken.

It's hard to imagine there was a time when she was closeted.

My mother reacted to our interview in the *Willamette Week* with the attitude of her era: that fools' names and fools' faces often appear in public places, repelled at the thought of our lives in a newspaper, something Jannine has had to get used to during the ten years I've written social commentary, fluff, and essays on family life that get pretty darned personal.

We didn't exactly go looking for the publicity, it met us halfway. While we were waiting at the County Building, Byron Beck, "Queer Window" columnist for the *Willamette Week*, was giving out business cards to couples willing to be interviewed after they got married. Jannine took a card, thought about it, and called him a few days after our reception. She figured, why not? The more people know about the same-sex couples who want legal marriage, the better.

Actually, Byron Beck chose another couple for his column: Darcelle, the publicly-spirited, philanthropic, iconic Portland drag queen (who has been married to a woman for decades), and his male life partner. They couldn't marry, but had a story to tell, nevertheless. However, Byron passed our number along to the "Hitched" columnist, and she came out with a *WW* photographer to talk with us in our home.

The picture they printed was horrible. Jannine looks pretty good, and the baby comes out smelling like a rose, but the rest of us have funny faces, our eyes squinting into the spring sun, looking ready to sneeze. Of course, it's not a beauty contest. The important part was being another set of faces (albeit goofy ones) people can picture in their minds when the subject of same-sex marriage comes up. The more real we seem, the more difficult it is to demonize us, to say that we are *different*, and less worthy of equal rights for our relationships.

The article did reach a lot of people, as evidenced by the sudden increase in felicitations coming in.

All the couples we know who got married March 3rd have been engulfed with good will. They were shocked at the continuing support in the form of hugs, greeting cards, gifts, and flowers, from friends, from neighbors, from acquaintances, and from strangers who somehow discovered the news. One friend received an e-mail from her brother after being on the news, and she hadn't heard from him in years.

Jannine thinks they "get it." She thinks that same-sex marriage suddenly being granted in Multnomah County made it just as suddenly apparent that we'd never been able to before. Over the years, we've had well meaning friends and family assume we could get married somewhere. When same-sex marriage came up, they'd say, "But you're married, right?"

"No."

"But you can get married in Vermont?"

"Umm, no, they have civil unions."

"Didn't Hawaii pass same-sex marriage?"

"No."

"You could get married in Canada."

"But it wouldn't count here."

"Oh …"

They didn't get it that we simply couldn't get married in any way that was recognized in the United States. We weren't making some counterculture choice to live together in sin to protest the inherent sexism of traditional marriage, to protect ourselves from increased taxes, or to avoid getting too comfortable in the relationship. When the reality of same-sex marriage arrived, they woke up to what we'd been denied.

They didn't consider, as the anti-same-sex marriage camp would have the voting public believe, that our marriage threatened their heterosexual marriages. As Lynn Bacon, the former Director of Children's Religious Education at the First Unitarian Church, said after the weddings on March 3rd, if any straight marriage should be threatened, it's hers. She went to seven same-sex marriages the first day they were offered, and says her marriage is just fine!

An Errand at Tiffany's

Jannine got to state her marital status for the first time when she ordered her temporary work visa for India, the gay man on the other end of the phone saying, "Right on," when she said "Yes, I'm married," and explained that she'd married me in March.

I wasn't thrilled with the timing of this trip.

It was to have been earlier, which might have had her out of the country just when same-sex marriage was offered, leaving me stranded at the alter. But, the trip was falling just as we were recovering from getting married, holding a reception, hosting my cousin, Dov, for spring break, and from another bout of seasonal illness. Plus, I was developing a strange new anxiety disorder about driving that left me shaking at the wheel. Three weeks seemed a long time for my wife to be away.

Not that I'm not used to being *on duty* for weeks at a time. I'm the "mom in charge," as well as the "mom of choice" most of the time, though Jannine has been the popular mom from time to time, and being the "dog meat mom" takes some getting used to.

I was more worried about her: three weeks in a country with a twelve hour time difference, malaria, dysentery, political upheaval, and a culture that does not appreciate no-nonsense women in pants. I wasn't sure she would be culturally accepted, no matter her degree of technical skill, as she set about training people in India to take over her job.

But like it or not, she was going.

Jannine generally depends on me to pack for her when she travels (since she tends to be working up to the minute we walk out the door), but in this case, I simply couldn't. I was up to my eyeballs with a one year-old, a nine year-old, and a budding adolescent set on knocking me off my pedestal; I didn't have time to facilitate her travel needs.

Jannine made lists, got shots, and ordered meds, just in case. But then there were the clothes: she needed me to help determine what she could get away with, and what would brand her a diesel dyke the moment she landed. While my mind was on other matters, I helped her shop online for something to wear in India.

My mind was on wedding rings.

We've had a few rings over the years, concrete symbols of intention that we could have, unlike the right to marry. We bought our first set of rings nine months after we fell in love, simple twisted gold bands we still wore.

Our second pair celebrated the purchase of our ugly condo in Kent, wider gold bands, to indicate our continued resolve to succeed as a couple despite being given two coffee makers at Christmas "just in case."

For our ninth Valentine's Day, I had a seriously substantial gold band inscribed for Jannine, and for our tenth anniversary Jannine had a family ring made-over into a ring I'd seen in an advertisement. It looked good when Jannine got it in the mail (though it was the wrong size), but it trapped moisture, causing the skin on my finger to swell, redden, and peel off in layers.

For our fifteenth anniversary, we thought about having a celebration, but balked at the fuss, went out to dinner instead, and bought the matching platinum bands we used during our marriage ceremony.

Even after all that, I still longed for "the ring," though I didn't have any clear idea of what "the ring" might look like. I was obviously not a big rock kind of girl, heirloom rings aren't plentiful in the family (my sister-in-law was wearing the only one), and I didn't need a diamond just to have one. I searched Web sites shyly at night, switching windows if Jannine came in the room. I glanced in jewelry cases in the mall. I was cool with getting married in a flurry, without the dress, without the barefoot children (though they'd gladly have taken off their shoes if I'd asked), but the princess within wanted "the ring."

It was while we searched for sandals that it happened. Two days before leaving for India, Jannine hadn't found footwear she thought would be both practical, and feminine enough to promote peace. She needed to shoe shop, and wanted me to go along. Chris and Lisa watched the kids, and we drove downtown to a specialty shop to find comfortable sandals for the narrow-heeled, yet large of foot.

After finding sandals for a price they didn't aesthetically deserve, we were leaving the shopping center when Jannine caught me glancing at Tiffany & Company across the street.

"Let's go in," she said.

I'd been in Tiffany's once before, to see what a Tiffany's really looked like. I'd seen the advertisements in *Vogue* and *Vanity Fair*, I'd visited their Web site, and I'd bought into the Tiffany's mystique: the light blue box, the Audrey Hepburn/Truman Capote angle, the idea that a ring from Tiffany's was the ultimate, classy declaration of love.

I have to say, they train their salespeople well. At no time did I feel that condescending stare that occurs in expensive stores when a customer comes in who looks of meager means, which has been assumed about me before.

I was in a Wendy's getting a snack for the kids once, while waiting for Jiffy Lube to finish lubricating our car, wearing my favorite thrift-store corduroy coat, and the manager made double our order of fries and a burger appear on our tray, and discreetly (and sweetly) offered me free food because she thought I was destitute.

Got rid of that coat fast.

But the Tiffany's people smiled, greeted Jannine and me, didn't come on too strong, or ignore us as insignificant. We strolled around the store, looked in every case, almost stalking our way over to the engagement rings. Jannine urged me to try some on.

"You'll never know if you don't try them on."

She was willing to go all out, go into debt, buy a rock, whatever would make it right to me. I tried on square cuts that made me feel pretentious, solitaires that seemed suburban, and modern designs more suited to someone in their sixties, having a gaudy good time, than a sentimental wife in need of a symbol.

At the very end of our loop around Tiffany's, we came to a design I'd seen on their Web site during my nocturnal browsing. Jannine said, "Try it on." It was a perfect fit. It was comfortable. It felt right. It wouldn't make the skin peel off my finger in scaly, dead layers. And it had five small diamonds.

"One for every member of our family," I said, looking at Jannine.

I wore it out of the store, and into the rainy afternoon, almost weeping that something so silly, so materialistic, so superfluous, could mean so much.

One Bad Experience

It was over a month later that we had our first jarring experience. It was our pediatrician—now our former pediatrician—who was seeing Duncan for a bizarre incident when, for no apparent reason, he fainted in class. The doctor, who I had liked previously, examined him, looked in his eyes, tested his reflexes, prodded him in the stomach, and declared him fit as a fiddle.

During the examination, the doctor asked how much television he watched, and she was thrilled that he watched almost none (pediatrician's love this), high-fived him, and we would probably have gone away content, except that Duncan said, "We've seen more television lately, because of the news, and being on the news," which meant telling the doctor that we'd gotten married; no big deal, I thought. She smiled, said she'd wondered if she'd see anyone she knew on the news, and that she hadn't seen us.

Then I told her, casually, that the protesters had really upset Duncan. She stiffened, saying, "Well, they have a right to their opinion." I didn't know what to say; that was true, and no one had tried to stop them. The one man had held a sign, unimpeded, and the other had screamed vile things at us, coming within inches, scaring us, and we said nothing. The doctor went on, speaking directly to Duncan. "You'll just have to think about it for yourself, over time, and decide for yourself if you think they're right or not."

Duncan was confused. He'd heard the protesters; how could she be asking whether or not he agreed with a person who was yelling, "Why don't you marry your dog?" The nurse, who was in the room during this episode, chuckled, and said, "I think you're going over his head. He'll get it in a few years." As if he was a little child, and not a twelve year-old with a brain.

Angry now, I told the nurse, "I think he's already had the opportunity to show the courage of his convictions."

We hastily concluded the visit, and I stewed on it for a week.

I thought about the assumptions the doctor and nurse seemed to imply. That Duncan wasn't allowed to make up his mind for himself and was being goose-stepped toward gay liberation, and that the protesters were somehow oppressed by Duncan's feelings. Did the doctor really imagine that what upset him was a

117

difference of opinion? That the protesters had stood there silently? That they'd chanted, "No gay marriage," or even, "Save the sanctity of marriage for straights," statements that would have upset no one and expressed the same political or moral viewpoint? Did she feel that Duncan wasn't allowed to be upset that someone had screamed hate at his parents, for hours, while we waited peacefully to take advantage of the Multnomah County Commissioners' decision? That somehow the protesters' rights were being denied, despite this being the first time in Multnomah County, and almost the country, that we have won on this issue?

We decided to change pediatricians. While she has every right to a differing opinion, would we want a doctor who, from her position of authority, suggests to our son that he question our equality?

I Have a Dream

While Jannine was in India, Anna was in the third grade play.

At our school, the third grade play is a combination of history, social studies, and music written by a visiting artist paid with the money earned by "Run For the Arts," a program in which all the children in the school run around the block, getting pledges based on how many laps they run, or in some cases, nice tidy lump sums. There tend to be a few skinned knees, but it works. Without it there is no arts program, and as the whole country learned in 2003, thanks to "Doonesbury," we barely have an education budget in Oregon, and it just keeps getting smaller ...

But that's another story.

In Anna's class, the kids were studying Portland history and landmarks (bridges, stumps, shipbuilding), and the social changes that have occurred since the city was founded. As I watched the third grade play, Graeme safely home with Marty and Terri, and Duncan by my side, I thought to myself, "I wonder ..."

Because besides putting on lively skits with songs about lazy pioneer men (thus the Portland moniker "Stumptown," they cut down the trees, but left the stumps), and one on women's suffrage that brought down the house, the kids did a skit about the Japanese internment during World War Two, and one on the Vietnam War. The former focusing on the tragedy of the Japanese who lost their livelihoods, homes, and families when they were taken from the West Coast and interned inland, the latter a re-enacted protest march that included a small-scale version of the Vietnam War Memorial onstage.

Kids love to dress as hippies.

I wondered: will our kids go to plays like these as the parents of elementary students, and one of the skits show two men or two women getting married? Will school children studying American history cover the Gay Rights Movement, specifically the decade in which equal rights were finally won with the right to marry?

I think it's possible.

Massachusetts was marrying same-sex couples at that moment, despite great efforts to derail that decision. Multnomah County had stopped issuing marriage licenses, but it had taken the issue to the legislators, who were to decide how to reconcile state statutes (which defined marriage as between a man and a woman), with the Oregon constitution, which only limited marriage to adults over the age of seventeen, and specifically demands the equality of all Oregonians.

Our presidential candidates in the upcoming election were actually discussing same-sex marriage and civil unions in polite terms, and weren't avoiding it like the plague, for fear of being tainted by the issue.

The kids in the third grade play doing a falsetto version of "Where Have All the Flowers Gone?" that made the audience simultaneously wince, smile, and tear up, may be hard pressed to understand the fuss about same-sex marriage when they reach voting age in ten years' time. The millions of children of gays and lesbians playing soccer, and baseball, and Barbie with the millions of children of straight families, are more likely to favor gay marriage as they grow up, having witnessed firsthand that same-sex couples are no big deal and just as boring as any other parents.

As I applauded at the end of Anna's play, I thought of a future in which eight and nine year-old kids will dress in drag for the third grade play, to mark the Stonewall riots at the beginning of the gay rights movement, much like Rosa Parks or Martin Luther King, Jr. symbolize the civil rights movement. I imagined a nine year-old girl in a surplice standing in front of two nine year-old boys or girls, with a big map of Multnomah County in the background, the scene (complete with vows, an exchange of rings, and an air kiss) greeted by a combination of applause and silence, just as the Vietnam War protest skit was received.

It will be part of America's history. I have a dream.

"Queers Should Be Able to Screw-up This Institution, Too"

Just after school let out for the summer, I took a much needed writing weekend/sanity break at the Doubletree Inn a mile from where we live. It was an unimaginable luxury, yet essential to surviving the summer with three kids twenty-four/seven, an ever-increasing driving phobia that had me scared on the freeway, even in the passenger seat, and a writing career I didn't want to put on hiatus for ninety days while I hosted a continuous stream of sleepovers at our house.

During a well-earned break from the my laptop (it was astounding what I could get done when I wasn't writing during naptime in the minivan or worrying about what to feed everyone for dinner), I went to Barnes & Noble, where I took a child-free cruise down the aisles, lingering deliciously over the novels, stopping at attention grabbing titles, and enjoying the luxury of shopping rather than making a swift purchase before someone blew a gasket.

I found myself in the "Gay & Lesbian" aisle, checking out the new books on same-sex marriage, four volumes hot off the presses. And beneath one of them, Jonathan Rauch's *Gay Marriage, Why it is Good for Gays, Good for Straights, and Good for America,* was an "employee recommended" card, giving a 20% discount off that title. When I looked closer, I saw that on the card was written, "Queers should be able to screw up this institution, too," signed Nick.

I stood there, perplexed.

I wasn't sure whether to complain about the irreverent language (was Nick queer identified? queer friendly? or was queer being used in a derogatory sense?), be glad that consumers were given an economic incentive to read a positive take on same-sex marriage, be annoyed—as a writer—that Nick didn't bother to actually say anything about Rauch's book that would inform a potential reader of its merits, or scream with rage that something gay and lesbian Americans have been denied was dismissed so cavalierly.

I did none of the above, bought a pair of reading glasses (my aging eyes feeling the wear and tear of a marathon writing session), and left the store otherwise empty handed, returning to room service and my laptop.

Retelling it later to my friend, Megan, she blew my socks off by saying Nick was absolutely right, "You should be able to screw up that institution, too!" She thought it was a rational argument in an irrational situation.

I guess she and Nick have a point: we should have the same right to mess up, trivialize, or take lightly the institution of marriage, the same as any other couple who jumps into matrimony with both eyes shut.

However much I think of marriage as a serious commitment, an expression of love, a contract to keep going even when the going gets tough, and a legal safety net as a couple, it is also a freedom of choice enjoyed by other adult Americans that has not been ours to make. And since freedom of choice is what made America "America," instead of a British colony 150 years after my ancestors lost their way to Plymouth Rock, and landed in Connecticut, maybe this argument is what will bring us marriage in the long run.

Gay and lesbian couples are never going to convince everyone that we're benign, law-abiding, church-going citizens about as scary as Bambi's mother, nor should we have to. There will never be a 100% consensus that we have the right to life, liberty, and the pursuit of happiness, if that includes marriage. There will always be folks who believe we're going to hell in a hand basket and good riddance.

But our laws don't usually require a consensus.

The battle over same-sex marriage was raging in Oregon: those opposed gathering signatures at churches across the state to bring a constitutional amendment banning same-sex marriage to the November ballot, making any more same-sex marriages an impossibility, and *Basic Rights Oregon* was fundraising in case the amendment made the ballot and they needed to make a push to reach voters before November.

More and more, as same-sex couples seek the right to marry, judges will have to ask themselves: is there a compelling reason to discriminate based on sexual orientation? Do the couples deserve equal rights? Are they in some way innately inferior and therefore ineligible to arm themselves with the protection of marriage for their committed relationships, with all the legal advantages that offers?

Conservatives called people like King County Superior Judge William L. Downing, who ruled in King County that DOMA was unconstitutional in Washington State, and Agnes Sowle, the attorney who wrote the recommendation that spurred same-sex marriage in Multnomah County, "activists," but they were merely interpreting the law without prejudice, a pretty challenging job. And no doubt a thankless one.

More and more, legal experts were recognizing as Nick, the Barnes & Noble employee, did, that we should have equal access to screwing up, taking for granted, or doing exceptionally well at the institution of marriage.

Fall into Stress

In late August, I joined the medicated masses, and gave myself up to a higher power—Paxil.

Sure, I was a little stressed-out about our country being on the brink of possibly re-electing the worst president during my lifetime, and that same president embroiling us in a war that can't seem to be won, with money our country can't afford, resulting in a loss of respect internationally that our children will have to reckon with.

True, it was a major bummer that our home state was fifty-fifty in the polls on whether Jannine and I would still be married on January one, and on whether we were worthy of that institution in the first place.

Surprisingly, I didn't let the Godzilla of common colds Anna brought home one week into September (which wiped out her next two weeks of school, Duncan's attendance record, and sank Graeme into a mucous-fueled manic phase that had him running at the nose and into the walls), knock me for a loop—though it did knock out my hearing, smell, and sense of taste for two weeks.

Nope, it was driving anxiety that had me running to the doctor, saying, "Give me drugs," so I could keep on trucking.

I'm sure it was an amalgamation of a lot of things, including all of the above, a wakeful toddler, no alone time, too much Diet Coke, and the large blind spots to the rear left and right of our minivan compared to the 360 degree view from the wheel of our former Jeep Wagoneer. I could drive small streets during daylight, I could even do them at night with a white knuckle grip on the wheel, but the freeway had become a break-out-in-a-cold-sweat nightmare.

I'd never been what you would call a confident driver. Jannine taught me when I was twenty-five; I'd decided not to get a license after passing Traffic Ed in high school since I was taking recreational drugs, and didn't think I was responsible enough to be behind the wheel of a lethal weapon. By the time I'd ended my flirtation with illegal substances six months later, I was in college, with no money, so driving was low on the priority list, and remained there until Jannine gave me lessons, having tired of the role of chauffeur in the relationship.

I'm normally a decent—if anxious—driver. I've never had a ticket, and the one time I was in an accident, I was the third car in a four-car pile-up on the freeway, when unaccountably, traffic came to a dead stop. I stopped in plenty of time, as did the car before me. It was the fourth car who plowed the rest of us into one another. The three other cars drove away, ours was totaled.

But August took me over the edge. It was Duncan's weeklong computer camp that did it. The hours were such that both drop-off and pick-up were during rush hour traffic. The first day had me gripping the steering wheel like a vise. The second day had me dreaming of on-coming traffic. By the third day, every time I closed my eyes I saw speeding vehicles and head on collisions, not a good thing for a sleep deprived parent of three.

We survived the rest of the week by devising long alternative routes. I never wanted to drive on the freeway again, though time and medication have worked wonders, and I'd consider myself 95% cured.

I suspect that my inability to just relax and go with the flow of traffic also had something to do with reading the editorial pages daily, the pain of keeping up on the legal status of our marriage, and what felt like a continual public assault on our dignity.

Jannine dealt with it by refusing to read the paper, look at letters to the editor, or listen to me tell her the latest insulting commentary or even any positive polls. She'd practically put her hands over her ears and sing, "La, la, la," if I tried to read her a quote.

Every day, the *Oregonian* published letters objecting to calling same-sex marriage a civil rights issue, since, the writers charged, we had exactly the same rights to marry as anyone else: we could marry someone of the opposite sex. We just couldn't marry the one we loved.

To me, the parallels with anti-miscegenation laws were undeniable: blacks could marry, whites could marry; they just couldn't marry each other.

The newspaper was bad enough, but being a neighborhood poster couple for same-sex marriage was getting tough, too; congratulations were a thing of the past, now we were walking, talking symbols of social debate. We couldn't go anywhere without the subject of legal same-sex marriage coming up; it was in the news, it was on the collective brain, but sometimes I felt like shouting, "This is not an intellectual exercise, people!"

They meant well. My mother, telling me we'd see legalized same-sex marriage in her lifetime, even if the constitutional amendment in Oregon passed in November, was trying to be supportive, even if "in her lifetime" might mean another forty years. My friend Cathy, stopping me in the hall at Alameda School, assured me she felt like Multnomah County did the right thing issuing marriage licenses to same-sex couples, but she wasn't so sure about the process, about County Commissioner Lonnie Roberts being left out of the decision, about not holding public debate prior to issuing licenses, and maybe about whether the decision was premature. I breathed slowly, I smiled, I kept my mouth shut, but I wanted to remind her (OK, scream at her) that this wasn't Sociology 200 or Political Science 101; this was my life, the lives of thousands locally, and millions across the country, being roasted on the barbeque pit of public debate.

In sarcastic moods, after reading another editorial suggesting same-sex marriage be put on hold "for the good of society," I would mumble to myself, fine, let those people imagine themselves in love with someone they were denied the right to marry. Let them imagine living for decades knowing their union is considered less than worthy of recognition, flouting society—if they dared—to love lawlessly for a lifetime, only to be denied access when their loved one is dying, denied the right to make medical decisions, to bury that loved one, or even to take bereavement leave, because legally speaking, the relationship was non-existent. See how they like it.

I mean seriously, we, the three thousand same-sex couples who married in Multnomah County, would have needed incredibly low self-esteem to not leap at the opportunity to legally recognize our commitments for what they are: marriages. We would have had to believe, like opponents of gay marriage, that we are not people capable or worthy of commitment.

When the window of opportunity opened, Jannine and I stepped over the sill. We knew that we might land in a legal quagmire, that our marriage license might be so full of legal loopholes, it could serve as a sieve, or that we could wake up the next day with the governor declaring the three thousand marriages illegal under state law.

Stress, editorials, and hallway debates aside, we were glad we did it. Not only because getting married is meaningful, even after seventeen years, three kids, and a mortgage, but because we were so glad not to wait another day for our marriage to be equal in the eyes of the law.

Paxil is a small price to pay.

A Devastating Election

The day after the November election, my neighbor, Chris, a white, able, middle-class gay man, marched across the street when he saw me dragging in my yard debris cans, and told me that for the first time in his entire life, he felt oppressed. He said that we had clearly been told to get to the back of the bus. And he was mad.

I started that Wednesday like so many, numb with disbelief, almost in denial. I'd turned off the television and gone to bed by nine on election night, already fried emotionally, and eager to avoid watching the seemingly inevitable re-election of George W. Bush, and the possible passage of Measure 36, constitutionally barring same-sex marriage in Oregon. In the morning, I opened my *Oregonian* to find that my home state, the state I love, did not love me. Our state constitution was amended to ensure that couples like us would never enjoy the benefits of marriage.

Bush, I tried to ignore, hoping recounts would throw him out of office, even if Kerry did concede.

Since I didn't start the day drinking highballs, the numbness wore off and emotion set in: first, in the form of tears, when our friend, Jason, e-mailed us to say that he would always think of us as married, that we were married, and that no one could take that away, then, like my neighbor, in the form of anger. I started constructing editorial essays in my head as I paced from room to room, picking up childhood debris and dog toys on automatic pilot. So, when journalist Bill Graves called wanting a reaction to the news that Measure 36 passed, he got an earful.

My primary argument has always been that denying gay men and lesbians the right to marry makes us less than second class citizens; it marks us as separate from the human race. An argument that the protester affirmed last spring as he screamed, "Why don't you marry your dog?" while we waited peacefully in line for our marriage license. But the other point I made to that reporter (but didn't end up in print) was what I think constitutional amendments banning same-sex marriage do to gay and lesbian youth.

It was one thing for me, in an almost eighteen-year relationship, to be outraged that once again the majority felt it had the right to systematically discriminate against me, and my family. It is quite another for a fourteen or fifteen year-old, just coming out, to get the message, loud and clear, that he or she is considered—by the majority—unworthy of marriage.

For some, this message will spur them to become happy, productive adults, despite this collective vote of no confidence. But, I imagine, more will internalize that message, be more suicidal, more promiscuous, and more inclined to stuff their feelings in a bottle of beer or the next ecstasy high.

The election hit us harder than I let on to the reporter, and much harder than we allowed the *Oregonian* photographer to see when he came by that afternoon and photographed us playing with Graeme on our dining room floor. Polls had shown Kerry winning the presidential election and the constitutional amendment losing, only the day before, lending us an optimism that was dashed to pieces as the early election returns came in.

While I wanted to bounce back fast and keep on fighting for marriage, there was a part of me so hurt by the voters who drew the line between us and them, that it was hard to recover from, and go about the day, the next day, and the weeks to come, knowing that we were legally enshrined as less; the possibility of our marriages so threatening they needed to be voted out of existence.

We went through a lot of chocolate as I recall.

The part of Jannine that opened up and flowered with our wedding, our celebration, and the community that embraced us after all these years (transcending the survival strategies she'd learned as a military brat to keep her guard up and her circle small), closed, withered, and barred the door.

That part of me that had felt at one with our neighborhood, our village, all at once felt alien and alone. The rebel from 1986 wanted to resurface in black leather, and say "screw you," since it seemed obvious that being a good sport, a good citizen, and Carol Brady in blue jeans had done nothing to change our status as "other."

There was a deafening silence at school for the week after the election. Silence from those who secretly voted with hearts and agendas that disagreed with ours. Silence from those who understood that words couldn't fix the damage or close the wounds that were still weeping quietly while other people went about their lives.

Anna's teacher, our friend Diane, pulled me into a hug the day after the election, holding me tight before asking what Measure 36 would mean for our own marriage.

"They can't take that away from you can they?" she asked. "You're already married!"

We still didn't know whether the state would let our marriage stand, it was going to the Oregon Supreme Court.

The First Wedding Anniversary

March 3rd, 2005, fell on a school day, much to our children's dismay.

There had been talk, when we were giddy with marriage and anything seemed possible, of all the kids celebrating our anniversary, too, of them gathering for laser tag, sumptuous feasts, maybe a day off from school? They'd been jazzed about our marriages, which were, in part, about them: to protect them, to celebrate them, to make them "legitimate."

As the day approached, it became clear that all the other mothers had reneged on this arrangement except us. We might still have been mavericks and let them hang at home that day and party the night away, except that Anna had missed two weeks of school for an undefined illness, and someone had to baby sit Graeme while Jannine and I celebrated … So Duncan and Anna had school as usual.

The Brides of March, as we came to call ourselves, all went out to dinner together, ten friends who had married that Wednesday at the First Unitarian Church, five couples who, in the joy, turmoil, and heartbreak after, had forged stronger friendships and appreciation for both our differences and our commonalities.

As moms, none of us get out much, but we'd had a trial run of sorts on New Year's Eve, going en masse to a lesbian dance and fundraiser. We'd brought with us a spirit of *joie de vivre* which had all of us dancing: Chris and Lisa two-stepping all over the floor, Jeanna and Ellen disregarding the beat in favor of slow dancing, and Marty and Terri doing an impromptu Waltz. Later, Chris cleared our table and patted it, urging me up. When Lisa told me to take advantage of this rare opportunity, "Come on Beren, it must be fifteen years since you've danced on a table," and the whole group urged me on, I did as I was told, and another couple of women followed suit on their own tables, since it really is fun up there, and something everyone should try.

I even got tips.

For our anniversary night, we booked a long table at a restaurant owned by a woman who offered us a free champagne toast when she was told the occasion, and announced to us (and the whole restaurant) that she'd just gotten engaged to her girlfriend. It was posh, dark, savory scented, and had stupid food, but it was good to be there with nine other women who understood what it had taken to reach that day.

At the table behind us, a group of straight moms from our daughter's school were having drinks and discussing their book group selection (allegedly), while taking a break from the home fires. When she saw our long table, one of the moms, our friend Christie, asked us what miracle had brought us out on a school night? When Jannine told her, they toasted our marriages, smiles all around.

What Christie and her book group couldn't know, was that it had been both the pinnacle of joy, and bitterly painful, to have married amid the support and disdain of a bipolar nation.

In the days before we gathered for pan-seared pork and prime rib, Bill Graves, from the *Oregonian,* had called many of us to ask us how we felt as the anniversary approached, and what benefits we'd received from getting married. Some of the moms had given him examples of small benefits offered by businesses, or stories about announcing their marital status.

I'd waffled about calling him back after he left us a message (and Jannine was done talking to reporters), and never did. He knew there had been no real legal benefits. Despite our marriages being registered with the state, they were in an unprecedented legal limbo. Did he wonder if we had married membership at health clubs? The zoo? Or had to pay more on our taxes as a couple? Obviously there were no social security benefits, automatic inheritance, or any of the other perks married heterosexuals got gratis with a license to wed.

I'd been burned before after being quoted in the paper, and didn't need more ribbing from people who saw our marriage, and others like them, as publicity stunts, attention seeking, or as Barney Frank put it (regarding the marriages in San Francisco), "spectacle weddings," proving that he simply didn't get it about wanting to marry the one you love. My skin felt too thin.

Even the many people who did "get it," suddenly seeing what we'd been denied, were ready to move on, feeling that the same-sex marriage issue was over, not realizing that it was far from over for any of us around that table eating slices of first anniversary wedding cake from Helen Bernhard's and remembering that morning in March.

Long after the ten of us had finished eating we stood outside the restaurant in the warm spring night, talking about the miracle we shared, until our bodies demanded to be put to bed, even if our hearts were on emotional overdrive.

Has being married made a difference? It's hard to know. Is it a coincidence that we have come to a place where Jannine and I seem to love each other, care for each other, and work hard to be the best people we can be, more than ever before? Is it from being married that we have resolved old pains, rediscovered old joys, and forgiven ourselves and each other for past mistakes? We seem to look with more open eyes at daily miracles, at the beauty of clouds in a bright blue sky, at the startled laugh of a tickled child, at the calm of a weekday morning. Could a wedding do all that?

March 3rd, 2004, was our wedding day, come what may.

The Water Fountain
of Legal Marriage

April 14, 2005

I was foolishly optimistic as I drove Anna to school in the minivan that morning. While Jannine remained numbly pessimistic, I was nervous and excited about the Oregon Supreme Court decision on Li v. the State of Oregon, expected to be announced at eight o'clock that morning. During the drive, Anna and I discussed possible outcomes, the best being that Jannine and my marriage, and those of the other three thousand same-sex couples who married in Multnomah County, would be declared legal at last: an island of same-sex marriages surrounded by a constitutional amendment that denied the possibility of more.

The more likely possibility, I told her, was that since we married before Measure 36 passed, and the Oregon constitution specifically demands equality for all Oregonians, if our marriages were declared illegal, equality in the shape of civil unions would surely be mandated.

OK, Anna said, "So, what is a civil union, anyway?"

"Basically," I told her, "It lets same-sex couples have most of the rights and privileges of marriage, but calls it by another name, making it more palatable."

"But, that's like blacks in America before civil rights," she said, "The water fountains." I agreed. The best outcome of the court decision would be the legalization of our marriage for keeps, drinking from the same fountain; the next best scenario would be separate, but somewhat equal, water fountains.

She balked at that, separate being clearly unequal to her. I pointed out that before last spring, we didn't get to drink from the water fountain of marriage, period, no matter how long we'd been together, how many taxes we paid, or children we happily produced. Civil unions would be a step in the right direction. The worst outcome, I said, would be that we, the committed gay and lesbian couples of Oregon, would have no water fountain at all.

Sadly, the Supreme Court's decision did not come with running water, and I felt like a fool for having believed it might be self-evident that we deserved equal-

133

ity as citizens. First, the decision affirmed that after Measure 36 passed, marriage in Oregon was limited to opposite sex couples, then, that statutory law already existed when the licenses were issued that limited marriage to opposite sex couples (despite the Oregon Constitution requiring equal rights for all, which constitutional experts felt trumped a statute), and went on to say that the three thousand marriage licenses issued by Multnomah County were void at the time they were issued, and (essentially) weren't worth the paper they were printed on.

The Supreme Court didn't touch on the possibility of civil unions, saying it wasn't properly put before them, sidestepping the constitutionality of discrimination.

I had been so hopeful, gleefully following the issue on CNN. The day before the decision, Governor Kulongoski put his weight behind a civil union bill (perhaps he was foolishly optimistic, too), but without the possibility of same-sex marriage, thanks to Measure 36, will there be any impetus for lawmakers to move on civil unions?

It was a sad day at our house. It's not everyday your marriage is annulled without your desire or consent. Our friends who were married with us that day exchanged phone calls and e-mails of support, but besides a bone-crushing hug from our friend Ann, who attended the weddings, there was barely a murmur from friends or family, and none of our parents phoned.

To compound the pain, the *Oregonian* headlined the news with not only a small photo of a couple whose marriage had been annulled, but a big one of a gloating straight couple as well, with a sizable section on their relief that the same-sex marriages from the year before were "never legal."

Lisa said she felt like she should have the word "void" printed across her forehead. I was seriously considering donning a "Second-class Citizen" T-shirt on a regular basis. Anna said she wanted a T-shirt that read, "The state voided my moms' marriage," and was creating a line of political buttons up in her bedroom.

Sure, it is not the piece of paper that makes or breaks the marriage. Our marriage will exist without it, has existed without it, but it was safer and more celebrated with it, and it marked our full equality as citizens.

We still feel blessed to have drunk from the fountain of legal marriage, if even for a short time. It was truly magical to have enjoyed the same rite of passage that so many of our friends and family have enjoyed. The water was delicious, appreciated, and savored, as it only can be by someone who has long wished to take a drink.

More than Just
a Check in the Mail

May 7ᵗʰ, 2005

It speaks volumes when the government won't even take your money; a check arrived in the mail from Multnomah County, a sixty dollar refund of our marriage license fee paid a year ago, and held in fiscal limbo until Li v. State of Oregon decided the three thousand same-sex marriages were null, void, and legally nonexistent, resulting in our fee being spat back at us with a tersely worded explanation without so much as a "we regret to inform you."

You'd think that after being refused the right to marry or even be civilly united with each other for seventeen years, and then, after being given the opportunity to legally marry, to have that marriage publicly debated, voted against, and finally annulled by the state and declared legally nonexistent, as if they could wipe the memories of our marriage clean, we would be impervious to pain.

But getting our sixty dollars back made me cry.

Oh, I could have cried over a million other things that day: the pouring rain, my red and dripping nose, our two sons with pneumonia coughing on the couch, not enough time in the day to care for sick kids, an even sicker spouse (sleeping the afternoon away upstairs under a pile of blankets and a pound of dirty Kleenex), our numerous pets and my mental state; but I am made of tough stuff.

The check hammered home what I know unconsciously every day, that we, my love and I, are lesser citizens under the law; they won't even take our money, we are so unworthy.

Is it such a huge leap to understand that we are human, that we fall in love, hope, dream, and work for a future, just like any other two adults choosing to spend their lives together, 'til death do they part, forever and ever, amen? It is hard for me to understand why legal protections for our unions, for our children, for our intentions in terms of wills, property, hospital visitation, and custody, are denied us when it has been decades since we were officially stamped "normal" by the American Psychiatric Association, and declared just another healthy variation on the human animal.

Morally, we're trying to do the right thing: to quit living in sin and get married. Ethically, we're trying to meet our spousal and parental responsibilities by ensuring security in the relationship via legal protections. Socially, we are eager to strengthen the fabric of society by marrying within the arms of family, friends, community, and our church of choice. Where did we go wrong?

By being two women who fell in love with each other.

I wasn't the only formerly-married gay person crying over the mail. We heard through the grapevine that other couples were finding it just as bitter a pill to swallow. When we got a mailer from Tiffany & Company the next day, Jannine picked it up and muttered, "What, do they want your ring back, too?" And went on to grumble about whether Multnomah County expects all the merchants to refund the money they made from tuxedo rentals, flower arrangements, matching rings, wedding cakes, and lingerie as a result of all those licenses.

Not that the check from Multnomah County was really a refund. We didn't want our money back. We didn't return a faulty product; we had a perfectly lovely product, our legal marriage, ripped from us, and were then informed that we shouldn't have been allowed it in the first place, and even, perhaps, that this is what we get for daring to want it at all. It was enough to make a grown woman cry.

At What Price Equality?

July 2005

The hotel beds looked like a bomb had struck. Blankets were flung back, food containers perched precariously on the pillows, dirty clothes mixed with sheets, and a pee-soaked disposable diaper leaned against the bedstead. Ah, vacation with the family.

The gray morning light of Vancouver, British Columbia, filtered through the sheer curtains as Jannine and all three kids piled on top of one another in one bed, making a human pyramid while watching cartoons, and I monopolized the other with the morning *Vancouver Sun*. It was a minor miracle that we were there at all, both of us having little energy to make vacation plans (partly due to that lingering post-election depression), and Jannine simply didn't have time to plan anything, even though it was her long-awaited eight weeks' sabbatical, and something to treasure.

It was in a vacation state of mind that I leaned back against the pillows to look at Vancouver's newspaper, and saw that Canada had become the fourth nation in the world to legalize same-sex marriage on the day we arrived. How ironic.

We hadn't any intention of taking them up on the option.

We were already married to our friends, to our family, and a piece of paper from Canada would get us nowhere with the American government. The only way to benefit from the marriage certificate would be to leave our Portland home, our friends, pull our children out of school, pack up our worldly possessions, and move to Canada.

Right.

I didn't even want to tell Jannine, who had successfully engineered that human pyramid on the next bed, with her as the foundation and Graeme the crowning glory, something that as a safety queen I would normally decry, but chose to ignore because I can't be a spoilsport all the time. What good would it do to bring the subject of same-sex marriage up; we couldn't take advantage of it, unless we moved to Canada, which so far had been just another city (though more European), and filled with unapologetic smokers.

But as we stood on the deck of the ferry coming into Nanaimo, on Vancouver Island, for the next leg of our journey, I felt a stirring of "home."

The drive north to Campbell River was shorter than I had calculated, and the kids were still gushing over glimpses of rocky beach, basking harbor seals, and the sun glinting off the Georgia Strait, when we turned into the driveway of the Seadrift Resort, where I began my career as a memoirist by running down the road yelling, "My father's drunk!" until my mother caught me.

Jannine was justifiably uncertain about my desire to stay in a cabin at the small fishing resort my family once owned (replete with spiders, beach rats, and bad memories), when I proposed the idea. But she accepted my arguments: the former buildings had been razed, the beach alone was worth the location, and it would be good for the kids to see the place that had formed my overly-protective psyche, my love of nature, and my belief in the great circle of life in all its gory glory.

Our kids were so much more ready for it than I had been, in 1970, when I burst out of my grandparents' smoke-filled car upon arrival, raced down the gravel path to the shoreline, only to find yards of stinking seaweed and sand fleas.

We moved to Campbell River, British Columbia, from Los Angeles, California, where we lived in a ranch house in the Hollywood Hills with avocado shag carpeting, surrounded by other ranch houses, sage brush, coyotes, and cottontails. My sister was Jodi Foster's classmate (before she went on to that French school), and every kid wanted to be a star. Beaches were warm, sandy, and filled with people, not rocky, isolated, and knee-deep in kelp.

I didn't know then that when the tide was out, it revealed a sandbar for swimming, a community of seals sunning on the rocks, and a rocky point that went far out to sea, binoculars needed to see someone standing on the farthest tip, from the shore.

Duncan and Anna were in heaven. There were seaweed beds to slither through, kelp whips to snap, crabs to grab, tide pools to explore, logs to ride, and stones to skip, and when we crossed the Island Highway to show them the spot where I once caught frogs each summer, we found a doe and her fawns standing in the shade. The wildlife watching (for easy to please enthusiasts like us) was to die for: herons fishing, seals bellowing, fingerlings swimming, bald eagles overhead, garter snakes in the grass, and turkey vultures devouring a dead sea lion with a bullet hole through its skull, just down the beach.

So cool.

And if our youngest says I sawed the head off the decomposing sea lion with our older son's pocket knife, soaked it overnight in a 50% bleach solution so we could add it safely to our skull collection, and that it was "clean as a whistle" in the morning, he doesn't know what he's talking about.

With the tide out, Shelter Point was an ecological goldmine; we spotted every specimen in our guide book to coastal wildlife of British Columbia, including a still-born harbor seal among the species of starfish, chitons, and limpets clinging to the rocks.

No, we didn't take him home and have him stuffed.

On the beach where I once walked barefoot on the barnacles, taking tourists to dig for butter clams and collect oysters (they are abundant now, and toxic to man), I stretched out my arms and felt at one with the world. This was my religion: the rocks beneath my feet, the mountains across the strait, the sky filled with eagles, vultures, and gulls, and a government that recognized us as equal.

It was a little freaky when we discovered that Peter, the owner, was the man who bought the resort from my mother in 1978, at a lowball price suggested by our real estate agent, who'd informed him that my father was a psychotic drunk who'd left her in the lurch with two kids, and that she'd take anything. Nor was it reassuring when we realized that the tenants in the next cabin were on crack. But it was a solid week of beach exploration during the day, and *Harry Potter and the Half-blood Prince* aloud at night, and saner than any other week I spent at the Seadrift during my lifetime.

It was on Quadra Island, a community of three thousand former draft dodgers, left wingers, and ecologically minded artists a ten minute ferry ride from Campbell River, that Jannine and I started thinking about the move to Canada. She had twigged to the Vancouver headlines on legalized same-sex marriage, and couldn't stop thinking about it any more than I could. We drove off the car ferry to Quadra, down the two-lane road to the Quadra Resort (we were the only tenants, the owner being ambivalent about opening the resort that summer), where we fed apples to deer, watched kingfishers dive, herons fly by, and I thought about real estate prices and schools.

While Jannine took the older kids kayaking two days into our stay, I pushed Graeme in his stroller into the small real estate office down the road, and checked out the listings. The equity on our Portland home could purchase free and clear eight wooded acres with a pond, a four bedroom home, and a guest house. It was sickening to learn that the prices had doubled in the prior two years. I told the agent, an older woman with soft frosted hair, that I was just curious, that my partner and I had fallen in love with Quadra. She twinkled, and said, "Everything starts with an idea!" then paused, "You know, the first same-sex couple to marry in British Columbia live here on Quadra."

I told myself I wasn't just trying to run away. It wasn't like we'd never considered moving to Canada. Many of us mentioned the idea when same-sex marriage became a possibility up north, just as the south scurried to deny us the chance. Also, as the draft loomed in a shadowy future, we'd already been thinking about Canada, about peace protests, and conscientious objector status, and shooting our sons in the foot.

A friend has already offered a small caliber weapon for the job.

Canada seemed, at that moment, to have so much to offer: socialized medicine, a free press, a multi-party political system, and for me, the chance to relearn how to say "oot" and "aboot" as I did in my youth, creating a mixed-up accent of Canadian, Californian, and Pacific Northwest that had people speculating about my European origin for years.

My wife was both for, and completely against, the idea. In theory, it sounded grand: move to Quadra Island, grow organic vegetables, telecommute, and bicycle for transport through the 52 inches of annual rain. In practice, it could endanger her job, and would separate us from the friendships and family relationships we have worked so hard to nurture, especially as gas prices soar, making frequent visits a fantasy.

Though there *is* an airport in Campbell River …

Our kids were strongly opposed, despite deer in the backyard and eagles overhead. We had put down roots so they wouldn't share our disjointed childhoods. Our plan had worked, oh so well. They were deeply embedded in Portland, entwined with the community through hair-like strands of self, shared experience, commonalities, until these strands could weather a hurricane. But a move would tear them to shreds.

I justified my desire to move by telling myself that the kids needed more nature, less city, in their lives. That the chance to kayak, to hike, to see bear swimming, eagles feasting, and breathe fresh air, was worth more than living where I worried every time they left the house, humans scaring me far more than any wild animal. I also saw with my own eyes how well they were suited to the natural world. They were never bored.

More than that, we experienced several parental "paydays," those rare moments when you see all the work you've put into your kids and all the talent and brains they came into the world with, combine. For some parents, it might be a moment of exemplary politeness, a perfect piano sonata, or a report card lined with A's. For us, it was seeing our naturalists in action: Duncan and Anna sneaking up slowly on the vultures and eagles feasting on the sea lion, able to observe without disturbing the birds; it was Duncan inching his way out to the seals on the rocks, his body low to the ground, risking barnacles and bloodletting to see them up close and personal. It was the way they would look, but not disturb, pick up a snake, but put it down exactly where they found it.

They loved that when an eagle eats a baby seal, it pulls its skin off, beginning with a cut in the tail, forming a sealskin bag that native Canadians would gather and use. They loved that killer whales were a few miles out to see, that bears swim between the Gulf Islands, and that just north of Campbell River, Vancouver Island was virtually wild, just logging roads, deer, black bears, and cougars.

They seemed to belong there.

Quadra Island is paradise in the summer (but doubtless depressing in the winter with those 52 inches of rain), but mostly I was still mad about our marriage being annulled. In that mood, I could not think of one person who kept me tied to home. Our house was just a house, something that could be replaced. I was angry that the entire nation wasn't outraged that our right to marry was put to a vote.

It was hard to re-enter America, to explain to the customs agent that they were all "our" children when she asked which children belonged to whom (though it would have been harder to explain that hypothetical sea lion skull and a few of our other unusual souvenirs), and drive the freeway south. Our future felt precariously balanced on a scale: our current life on one side as second class citizens under the law and a life with equality, and the unknown, on the other. We asked ourselves, when does it cost too much in human dignity to stay? When have you pounded your head against a brick wall too many times? When is it worth uprooting a family and beginning a new life?

Back in Portland, it took weeks to feel "at home," to grow back in love with our pink stove, the Martha Stewart Naples Yellow paint on the walls, the framed memories lining the stairs, the drawings, the photos, the vintage cameras, and antique typewriters, the furniture begged, borrowed, and stolen (*long* story) but never new, that make up our domestic world. It took weeks to readjust my dial to Portland time and space; my mind was on Quadra, with equal rights and bald eagles, not on back-to-school supplies or registering Duncan for online math.

It was on Anna's first day back at Alameda in September that I felt I could stay. As I walked across the brick courtyard to the playground, greeting old friends, recent acquaintances, and former teachers while Graeme ran ahead to climb the play structure, I thought, "These are my people. Portland is my home. It's worth fighting for."

The scales are tipped, for now.

No More Mrs. Nice Gay

Her name was Alice, a Generation X razor-cut blonde with her Wonderland namesake illustrated over her upper arm, and she was holding my wrist down with an iron grip surprising in a person so petite and fragile appearing. But then again, it was her job to restrain the body part in question so that the ink didn't stray off course, creating a tattoo no one would be happy with, and wouldn't enhance my body or her reputation. Besides, she was a mom, and motherhood isn't for wimps.

Laurie was there to metaphorically hold my hand; physically, she was sitting in a chair nearby working on her laptop, updating the business cards she'd designed for me (one for my writing, one for my painting), and then working on a project for her graphic design business. As a single mother, she's developed the ability to work anywhere, anytime, even in a tattoo parlor. She looked up from the computer screen long enough to give her approval to the tattoo design, discuss placement, and take a few pictures of the process, so that Jannine and the kids could see what it looked like getting inked.

Jannine was on a business trip for the day, or I might have had some real hand holding, though compared to childbirth, tattooing is a tickle.

No one but me, and Alice, knew what I'd be getting that day, a Celtic triple spiral that serves double symbolic duty, representing both our three kids and the three stages of womanhood: maiden/mother/crone. I'd been waffling about getting another tattoo for almost twenty years, the patterns of hieroglyphics on my under wrists relics of my early twenties and not regretted. I'd wanted three new tattoos, one in honor of each child (two suns and an earth?), and visited a tattoo place in the neighborhood to ask about help designing what I had in mind, only to be referred elsewhere by the artist, a long-haired hipster in his early thirties who had been interested in helping me on previous visits to his establishment. Since then, I'd cut my long, wavy, positively pre-Raphaelite hair short. He was no longer interested in being of assistance.

Coincidence? I think not.

Guys liked the hair. Aging hippies tried to pick me up in pet stores with my wife standing by. I got great service at the gas station, despite being middle-aged. Waiters brought me extra bread. But lesbians looked right through me.

I didn't cut my hair to spite the guys or attract the girls, I cut it mostly for Jannine, who likes it short, and because I was tired of being invisible as a lesbian. Maybe that's why I was getting the tattoo, pulling out my Doc Marten's, and wearing my retro reading glasses. Jannine joked that I was doing a total makeover and she'd be given the boot next.

As if she could get rid of me that easily!

It wasn't just that I was in serious need of a make-over, or that I'd had a bad hair summer, or that nobody's gaydar was going to find me in a million years, all of which partially applied.

Mostly, I was tired of being Mrs. Nice Gay, that sweet, unthreatening lesbian with the long hair, nice kids, white minivan, and too much lipstick.

It was while we were in Canada that I realized just how angry I was. I'd felt hurt, sad, disbelieving, and numb, but hadn't noticed the anger because I am uncomfortable with rage. In Canada, it became unavoidably evident why I was so angry: we were in a nation that rushed us to equal status, not based on our income, our merits, or how pretty we are, but on the basis that it was the right thing to do. The Prime Minister of Canada made a speech stating that Canada was a nation made up of minorities, gays and lesbians among them, and the rights of one needed to be the rights of all.

Oh, Canada!

While we were enjoying the last of Jannine's sabbatical at Chris and Lisa's mountain cabin, the possibility of civil unions in Oregon died as well, at least for the next couple of years. *Basic Rights Oregon* had been campaigning for a bill that would pass anti-discrimination laws and civil unions for same-sex couples, and despite early indications that the bill would fail, they had managed to get the votes necessary to pass! But in what *Basic Rights Oregon* called the "Midday Massacre" of the bill, SB1000, Speaker of the House Karen Minnis threw out a 140 year-old rule that allowed legislators to extract a bill from committee and bring it to a vote. SB1000 never got the chance to pass.

Minnis's claim that legislators would be going against the will of the people by passing SB1000 doesn't hold water, since the majority of voters polled supported civil unions, even if they opposed same-sex marriage. The elected officials couldn't represent their constituencies and vote on civil unions.

How can our desire for legal representation be so threatening?

If we are a democracy, and not a meritocracy (or a beauty contest), my looking like a soccer mom in a lame attempt to get "a place at the table" isn't going to work any more than being exceptional has worked for the dozens of highly paid professional gays and lesbians who have been the poster people for gay rights over the last decade. Our lesbian friends (who include professors, 911 operators, a Vice President of Information Technology, midwives, therapists, and computer geeks), and even famous lesbians (Melissa Etheridge, Ellen DeGeneres, Martina Navratilova, and Mary Cheney) don't have legal parity any more than the blue collar bull dyke down the block working at Home Depot, a lumber mill, or pulling lattes late into the night, because we, as a class, are deemed unworthy of marriage.

I figure, why expend any more energy on not being me, when being "not me" didn't get me (or us) anywhere?

Not that I would ever be a clone of the bull dyke down the block (bless her hard-working heart), or regret the pre-Raphaelite hair (the jury is still out, I may grow it back), but the people who matter are broad enough to embrace a tattooed mama in horn rims, just as they could embrace a long-haired mom in Gortex. The mothers and fathers from Alameda School, the cousins from Eastern Washington, and the friends who gathered for our wedding reception and dropped off flowers, don't care what I look like. It was me who was editing, desperate to change the world by making myself palatable, an ambassador for the "everyday gay" to further the cause of legal marriage.

Jannine and I didn't expect our unprecedented joy to become the greatest sorrow our marriage has known. Jannine has yet to recover from the election results, the majority finding us unfit to marry still throwing her off her stride (is there a prescription drug that makes it more tolerable to be voted less than deserving of a legal union?), though she's begun taking photographs of objects other than angry bumper stickers, which is a good sign. The dull ache of depression that spread like a cancer through me over the last year (medication did help me drive, and did wonders with my anxiety over the holidays) was unexpressed anger at the insult hurled at us, undeserved.

Some have asked, "Why does it hurt so much to lose something you never had before, anyway?"

I can only say that our reaction seems to be universal. The couples we know who married on that rainy Wednesday, and in the brief legal window following, were devastated by the loss of their marriages, even though those partnerships, their non-legal marriages, had existed for many years. Lisa says she thinks the pain is because we dared to believe, we let ourselves take the leap of faith that our community would stand by us, uphold our legal equity, and let the marriages stand. Certainly there were bold statements made by straight friends and family that the state could not undo what it had already done, that once the licenses were granted, what could anyone do?

That our marriages would be annulled, against our will, didn't even occur to them.

Not that we are totally without a sense of humor about the situation. Jannine and I recently tried to watch a grown-up movie instead of *The Incredibles* (for the thousandth time), or *Scooby Doo and the Alien Invaders* (for the five hundredth time), and got *The Laws of Attraction*. As Jannine slipped in the DVD, I said, "Is this another movie about heterosexuals abusing the right to marry?"

She looked at the cover. "Yeah, it's going to really piss us off, isn't it?"

We watched it anyway. Julianne Moore. Wow.

We, Chris and Lisa, Marty and Terri, Jannine and I, three sets of brides who camped out to marry, will never say it was wrong to marry March 3rd. Those who bemoaned the quick action are probably still watching their televisions, patting themselves on the back for predicting that bad things would come of it. But since then California, Connecticut, and New Jersey have come closer to same-sex equality, catching the ideological wave sweeping the nation, demanding we be treated like people, not perverts. The tide of change may have receded in Oregon, but we were part of it, and don't regret it. I've had my wedding, and it was perfect, and can never be taken away.

My "No More Mrs. Nice Gay" mood coincides with our last year as Alameda moms, and both of us turning forty-one. One could suggest I'm in a second adolescence, perimenopausal, or inadequately medicated, but it merely means that I won't be candy coating my arguments, covering my soap box with embroidered appliqué, or aiming for unthreatening in the wardrobe department. My minivan is covered with political bumper stickers and my rainbow flag is flying.

Beware this Bride of March, I'm a tattooed lesbian wife and mother, make way.

The End

Epilogue

March 3, 2007

The Brides of March continue to consider themselves married, and have between them a combined total of three minivans, ten kids, six dogs, and ninety years of commitment.

About the Author

Beren deMotier graduated from the University of Washington Women's Studies Department in 1986, and put that degree to good use raising open-minded children and her readers' eyebrows as a social commentary/humor writer. She's written about life as a lesbian mom for *Curve, Greenlight.com, And Baby, Proud Parenting Magazine, Prideparenting.com, eHow.com,* on her Web site, <u>www.berendemotier.com</u>, and for newspapers across the country. She contributed to *The Complete Lesbian & Gay Parenting Guide* by Ari Istar Lev, published by Penguin in 2004.

When she's not up to her elbows in dishes, driving kids across town, playing Candy Land with her four year-old, or trying to find something funny to write about the flu, she paints portraits of dogs. She lives in a cozy, liberal enclave of Portland, Oregon, with her spouse of twenty years, their three children, and a Labrador.

Visit www.thebridesofmarch.com.

978-0-595-43987-4
0-595-43987-X

Printed in the United States
80455LV00006B/253-300